Unapologetically Me: Embrace Your Authentic Power and Self Love

Leon McCoy

Published by Leo Vinci, 2024.

While every precaution has been taken in the preparation of this book, the publisher assumes no responsibility for errors or omissions, or for damages resulting from the use of the information contained herein.

UNAPOLOGETICALLY ME: EMBRACE YOUR AUTHENTIC POWER AND SELF LOVE

First edition. November 2, 2024.

Copyright © 2024 Leon McCoy.

ISBN: 979-8227166449

Written by Leon McCoy.

Also by Leon McCoy

Unshakable: Build Lasting Confidence And Conquer Your Fears
Killing Lust Is Easy: A Journey Worth Taking
Rewiring Your Brain: A 100-Day Journey to Overcome Porn Addiction
Silence Is Power: How Quiet Leaders Dominate The Loud World
Beyond First Impressions: The Essential Guide To Building Meaningful Relationships
Mastering Your Potential: Breaking The Chains Of Limiting Habits
Unapologetically Me: Embrace Your Authentic Power and Self Love

Table of Contents

Introduction 1
Chapter 1 | The Power of Self-Expression 5
Chapter 2 | Embracing Your Uniqueness 14
Chapter 3 | From Self-Doubt to Self-Worth 23
Chapter 4 | Authenticity in Relationships 33
Chapter 5 | The Journey of Self-Love 44
Chapter 6 | Living Boldly, Without Apology 54
Conclusion 65
Appendix 69

Introduction

The path to self-acceptance might seem like an uphill fight in a society that frequently pushes us to shape ourselves to meet social norms. A lot of us are enmeshed in a vicious cycle of self-doubt, comparison, and the constant quest for perfection. We may doubt our value and give up on our true self as a result of the words of the outside world drowning out our inner truth. However, there is a profound truth hidden behind the layers of indoctrination and self-criticism: accepting who you are is essential to living a happy life and is not only a luxury.

"Unapologetically Me" is a plea to take back your story. It challenges you to investigate the deep relationship that exists between self-compassion, self-love, and the capacity to stand firmly in your own authority. This book aims to shed light on the process of accepting your true self, appreciating your own journey, and developing a greater awareness of your intrinsic value.

Self-love is not about narcissism or self-obsession, unlike what many people believe. As an alternative, it is the bold act of valuing oneself and treating yourself with the same love and care that you effortlessly show to others. Learning to put your needs and wants first might feel revolutionary in a culture that often exalts self-denial and self-sacrifice. The realization that you cannot pour from an empty cup is what causes this change, not selfishness. You can better assist and encourage others around you if you take care of yourself.

One of the most important pillars in this path is self-compassion, which is essential to navigating our flaws and mistakes. Instead than criticizing our difficulties harshly, it encourages us to approach them with compassion and understanding. Dr. Kristin Neff popularized the idea, which serves as a reminder that being human means having flaws. Everyone encounters sadness, disappointment, and pain; how we handle these situations is what counts.

By choosing self-compassion, we may accept our emotions without passing judgment, which promotes emotional health and resilience.

Another crucial step in this process is developing self-esteem. True self-worth originates from inside, although self-esteem can frequently feel ephemeral and be linked to accomplishments or approval from others. It's about realizing your inherent worth, regardless of your achievements, how you look, or what other people think. Unlearning damaging myths that have been engrained in us throughout time—often by well-meaning classmates, teachers, and caregivers—is part of this path. It involves changing your narrative and letting your inner guidance take precedence over the cacophony of self-doubt.

The purpose of this book is to walk you through the process of developing these essential components of self-acceptance. Every chapter will explore useful techniques, introspective activities, and uplifting revelations intended to assist you in discovering who you really are. Instead of offering a one-size-fits-all solution, the goal is to provide you tools that are relevant to your particular path.

You'll come across a number of themes as you go along, such as the value of being vulnerable in order to build connections, the transformational potential of creating boundaries, and the role that thankfulness plays in changing your perspective. You'll learn how social influences affect how we view ourselves and how to take back your story in a society that frequently tries to define you. The article aims to establish a feeling of shared experience by using realistic examples and personal tales to reaffirm that you are not facing this challenge alone.

You'll discover that it's okay to embrace your flaws and eccentricities in addition to your talents when you embrace your true self. Understanding that every aspect of who you are adds to the exquisite tapestry of who you are is part of this holistic approach to self-love. It's a call to delve deeply into your identity, encouraging curiosity rather than condemnation. This path invites you to embrace your whole self with all of its complexity rather than aiming for a flawless version of yourself.

In order to promote self-reflection and personal development, this book contains useful activities. These exercises are designed to help you confront negative thought habits, push yourself beyond your comfort zone, and promote self-discovery. Every practice helps you better comprehend self-love, from journaling questions that inspire introspection to guided visualizations that enable you to picture your most genuine self.

The significance of community is another important component of this investigation. Even while the path to self-acceptance can be quite personal, talking to others about your experiences and realizations can help you feel supported and like you belong. Creating a network of people who support and encourage you may be a tremendous source of inspiration and comfort. By working together, we can establish environments that value honesty and celebrate vulnerability.

Remember that the road to self-love is not a straight line as you turn the pages. It's a convoluted path with ups and downs, victories, and times of introspection. Sometimes you can feel like you're making progress, but then you'll find yourself struggling with self-doubt once again. Being kind to oneself during these times is crucial since this is a necessary step in the process. Every action you do, no matter how tiny, demonstrates your bravery and dedication to accepting who you are.

Recognizing the outside influences on our sense of self is equally essential. The environment around us might impose unreasonable norms that we can feel under pressure to match, such as professional requirements or cultural standards of beauty. The first step to freeing oneself from unwanted effects is acknowledging them. You give yourself the ability to establish your own criteria for success and value by confronting and questioning existing social conventions.

We will also examine the idea of authenticity in this setting. In a society that frequently praises conformity, it takes bravery to be true to yourself—the strength to tell your truth, to be vulnerable, and to accept your individuality. Being authentic is living in accordance with your values and ideas, not only expressing who you are. It entails maintaining your individuality in the face of outside pressure.

This journey is about removing the layers of conditioning and recovering the core of who you are, not about changing into someone else. It's about embracing your uniqueness and realizing that your uniqueness is what makes you unique. You will become more powerful in your own life and as an example to others if you embrace your authenticity more.

Remember that growth, not perfection, is the aim as you explore self-love, self-compassion, and self-esteem. In and of itself, every step toward self-acceptance is a win. Give yourself permission to make mistakes, develop, and learn. You will discover your inner power as a result of these events.

"Unapologetically Me" is ultimately about building a life in which you can be proud of who you are and what you stand for. It's about living fully, unashamedly, and genuinely. Take advantage of the chance to uncover your true potential and develop the love you so dearly deserve as you set off on this life-changing adventure. You have the ability to design a more vivid, satisfying existence for yourself, and every moment spent in self-discovery is a step in that direction.

Chapter 1
The Power of Self-Expression

Finding Your Voice in a World Full of Noise

It might be difficult to discover your voice in a world when social media, incessant alerts, and an endless stream of viewpoints are the norm. Our internal conversation is frequently drowned out by the clamor of outside stimuli, which causes many people to doubt their feelings, ideas, and desires. However, self-expression is more than just a way to communicate; it is a potent instrument for self-awareness and negotiating life's challenges. It enables us to connect with others, express our realities, and develop a deep sense of self-awareness.

Self-expression may take many different forms, such as written ideas, spoken words, creative activities, or simply basic body language. Every kind of expression provides a different way for us to discover and share who we are. We may gain a deeper understanding of our feelings, convictions, and values by using these channels. Anyone who wants to live an unashamed life and accept their true self must go on this path.

We frequently refrain from completely expressing ourselves out of fear of being judged. We could be concerned about how other people would interpret our ideas or perspectives. Our creativity and sincerity may be stifled by the crushing stillness that this concern may produce. However, it's crucial to acknowledge that everyone has the freedom to express their viewpoints and experiences. By speaking up for what we believe and feel, we not only affirm our own existence but also add to a larger dialogue that may encourage and elevate others.

Recognizing our limitations is the first step towards embracing self-expression. We frequently feel pressured to conform to societal conventions that govern how we should speak and act. Many of us are given subliminal cues on how to express ourselves from an early age. We could be taught to repress our rage, conceal our weaknesses, or write off our goals as unrealistic. We may become disconnected from our actual selves as a result of this indoctrination, which can make us feel alone and unauthentic.

It's critical to reflect on oneself in order to overcome these limitations. Examine your views on self-expression first. What anxieties come to mind when you consider sharing your ideas or creative output? Have you ever suppressed your voice because of any particular experiences? You may explore your feelings and spot trends in your behavior by keeping a journal, which can be a useful tool in this process. You may start to remove the obstacles preventing you from expressing yourself by becoming aware of these underlying anxieties.

Think about the several ways you may express yourself as you set out on your adventure. Even though verbal communication is preferred by many, other forms of communication can be just as effective. There are many ways to express your emotions and ideas, including writing, dancing, music, and art. You might discover secret facets of your individuality and feel liberated by trying out various ways of expression. Painting or sketching, for example, may provide a more natural means of expressing your inner world if you feel that words frequently elude you.

Safe and encouraging settings are ideal for creativity. Be in the company of people who support you in expressing your opinions without worrying about criticism. This encouraging group may create an environment that encourages self-expression. Take part in discussions that challenge your viewpoints and open your thinking. Workshops, discussion boards, and creative collectives are examples of collaborative environments that may encourage you to discover your voice and value the distinctive contributions you make.

It's important to establish routines that respect your self-expression in addition to looking for encouraging surroundings. You may let yourself know that your voice counts by scheduling specific time for creative endeavors. A weekly painting session where you focus on your creative process or a daily writing practice where you record your ideas without editing them may be examples of this. These customs act as a reminder of your dedication to self-awareness and sincerity.

Facing the inner critic that frequently lurks in the background is a crucial part of discovering your voice. This voice, which comes from fear and self-doubt, may be unrelenting in its criticism. It suggests that your feelings are too intense, your work is inadequate, or your thoughts are unworthy. Regaining your authority requires that you learn to identify and confront this internal discussion. Use affirmations of your value and the legitimacy of your experiences to combat these critical ideas as soon as you become aware of them. Keep in mind that self-expression is about being honest and genuine, not about being flawless.

Finding your voice can also be facilitated by paying attention to your instincts. We frequently ignore our intuition in favor of social norms or outside viewpoints. But developing a close relationship with your intuition enables you to identify what really speaks to you. To access your inner wisdom, practice mindfulness, meditation, and introspection. You can discover that your own voice emerges when you make time to listen, bringing to light concepts and insights you might have missed before.

Self-expression is by its very nature a vulnerable act. It takes guts to be honest about your feelings and views, especially in a society that sometimes prizes conformity over uniqueness. You may be able to speak more authentically if you acknowledge this weakness. Accept the discomfort that comes with being vulnerable; genuine connection frequently happens at these times. Giving oneself permission to be seen encourages others to follow suit, which spreads a culture of candor and openness.

Realizing that your voice has the ability to influence other people is also essential. You add to a shared story that may spur understanding and change every time you share your ideas and emotions. People who could be on similar routes might relate to your experiences, hardships, and victories. By speaking your truth, you give others who are struggling to find their voice hope in addition to confirming your own identity.

Taking part in community-focused initiatives or activism might help you express yourself more fully. You may make a significant difference and build relationships with people who share your values by using your voice to support issues that are important to you. Your voice may act as a catalyst for awareness and change, whether you choose to use it for writing, public speaking, or grassroots organizing. Your message will be more sincere and your resolve to live an unapologetic life will be strengthened if your self-expression is in line with your ideals.

Even while self-expression has great power, it's crucial to approach it mindfully. Think about how your words affect you and other people as you negotiate the challenges of speaking up. Self-expression should be a tool for development and connection rather than a way to release anger or project negativity. Make an effort to speak intentionally, aware that your voice matters and has the power to promote harmony or conflict.

It might be beneficial to review the reasons why self-expression is important to you during times of self-doubt. Think back to the times when speaking up has made you happy or encouraged relationships. Remembering these moments might help you stay motivated and encourage you to keep being honest. Keep in mind that each time you speak up, you are reaffirming that your voice matters and is worthwhile.

As you develop your self-expression skills, think about how storytelling might help you connect with others. We can effectively communicate our experiences, feelings, and insights via our tales. By sharing your personal story, you may build empathy and understanding. It allows people to enter your world and inspires them to consider their own paths. Storytelling, whether it be in writing, speech, or other forms of artistic expression, may highlight the universal themes that bind us all.

Be gentle with yourself as you embark on this self-expression path. Discovering your voice is a continuous process that involves development and progress. On some days, expressing oneself could come naturally, while on other days, there might be difficulties and barriers. Give yourself permission to handle these changes without passing judgment. No matter how it appears, every instance of self-expression advances your continuous quest for authenticity.

In the end, discovering your voice is a power reclaiming. In a society that frequently seeks to stifle originality, it represents your dedication to respecting your ideas, emotions, and personality. You develop a greater awareness of both the outside world and yourself by embracing self-expression. You give yourself the ability to stand up in your truth and navigate life with clarity and confidence.

Accept the depth of your experiences and the individuality of your voice as you delve into the subtleties of self-expression. Every idea, sensation, and thought you have together adds to the fabric of mankind. Your genuine voice is a priceless gift in a noisy society that should be appreciated, honored, and heard. Give yourself permission to embrace this power and see how living really and unashamedly may change your life.

The Art of Owning Your Identity

The act of self-expression turns into a strong declaration of uniqueness in a world where conformity is sometimes the norm. Owning your identity is accepting the many facets of your life and sharing them with the world, not just claiming to be who you are. We are encouraged to delve deeply into our experiences, values, and beliefs through this process of self-expression and self-discovery, which eventually equips us to live honestly.

The act of self-expression facilitates communication between our inner and outer selves. It enables us to communicate our ideas, feelings, and experiences in ways that are meaningful to both ourselves and other people. Because it promotes empathy, understanding, and the ties that bind us together as human beings, this connection is vital. When we have the guts to be real, we not only validate our own experiences but also encourage others to follow suit, spreading authenticity.

Investigating the idea of self-awareness is necessary to comprehend what it means to own your identity. This fundamental component enables us to consider the values, passions, and convictions that influence our perspective on the world. Journaling and mindfulness are two examples of introspective activities that can help us uncover the many facets of who we are. Through this investigation, we may learn about the experiences that have molded us—both the successes and the setbacks—and see how they have influenced who we are now.

When it comes to expressing yourself, many people struggle with the fear of being judged. This fear is frequently brought on by earlier encounters in which our feelings or views were disregarded or condemned. These experiences might make us reluctant to reveal who we really are, which can result in a safer but ultimately unsatisfying façade. One of the most important steps in taking back your voice is admitting and facing your concerns. You may feel more empowered and inclined to speak your truth when you realize that your experiences are real and worthy of being heard.

It takes time, patience, and effort to find your voice. Starting in low-pressure settings, such writing in a private diary or discussing ideas with a trusted friend, might be beneficial. You may express your emotions and gain confidence with this methodical technique, free from the burden of criticism from others. You could eventually find yourself sharing more freely in a variety of contexts, such as social media and group conversations, as you grow more at ease with self-expression.

Another effective way to take ownership of your identity is via artistic expression. The arts provide you a platform to express your feelings and ideas, whether via writing, dancing, painting, or music. Being creative can be a freeing experience that provides a way to communicate emotions that can be hard to put into words. Additionally, producing enables you to access your intuition and uncover facets of yourself that you may not have previously acknowledged.

In order to express oneself, one must also embrace vulnerability. It takes guts to be who you truly are, even when it makes you uncomfortable. Being vulnerable helps others connect with you and see you for who you really are. Sharing your own sentiments and opinions encourages others to do the same, fostering an accepting and open atmosphere. A stronger sense of belonging and deeper connections might result from this reciprocal vulnerability.

Establishing boundaries is essential to the process of becoming an identity owner. Setting and maintaining boundaries protects your mental health while enabling you to express who you are. You may foster an atmosphere that encourages your honesty by defining what seems right and wrong. This might be avoiding people who minimize your experiences or participating in conversations that respect your viewpoint. You may emphasize the value of your voice and your right to express it by maintaining your limits.

Your social and cultural identity might also be closely linked to how you express yourself. Our backgrounds have an impact on everyone of us, forming our viewpoints and life experiences. Examining these factors can help you better understand who you are and provide you a strong platform to communicate who you are. Honoring your ancestry while accepting your uniqueness may be achieved via connecting with it through storytelling, art, or community service.

Contradictions are common while navigating the complexity of identity. We might have to juggle a number of roles, including activist, professional, parent, and friend, each with its own set of demands. Harmonizing these aspects enables you to portray a whole picture of yourself, which is the art of self-expression. It's crucial to keep in mind that you are a dynamic synthesis of your experiences, convictions, and goals rather than being defined by any one element of who you are.

Storytelling is one of the most powerful methods to communicate who you are. Telling your story can shed light on the path that brought you to where you are now. You may digest your experiences and learn more about your life via this potentially therapeutic process. In addition to honoring your path, telling your story makes room for others to consider their own stories. People from different origins may connect via storytelling, which serves as a reminder of our common humanity.

Furthermore, advocacy might take the shape of self-expression. You exemplify your identity's power when you utilize your voice to defend oppressed populations or to speak out against injustice. Since advocacy brings your behaviors into line with your principles, it becomes a potent weapon for self-expression. By defending your convictions, you support a greater movement that promotes change in addition to affirming your personal identity. The idea that your voice counts and can have an impact is reinforced by the junction of activism and self-expression.

External obstacles are frequently encountered on the path to identity ownership. Our true selves and the expectations placed on us might clash as a result of societal influences that define how we should act, think, or appear. Regaining your individuality begins with acknowledging these forces. You open the door to a more satisfying life by defying social expectations and valuing your individuality.

It's crucial to approach the process of developing self-expression with compassion. Understand that it takes time to grow and that it's normal to encounter obstacles along the road. As you work through the challenges of expressing who you are, try to be nice to yourself rather than too hard on yourself. Honor your accomplishments, no matter how minor, and recognize the bravery required to be true to who you are.

Being around by encouraging people can help you on your path to self-expression. Look for communities, mentors, or friends who value uniqueness and promote candid communication. Interacting with others who have similar beliefs to your own may help you feel validated and like you belong, which can create an atmosphere that encourages self-expression. These relationships serve as a reminder that your voice matters and that you are not traveling alone.

Think about the value of consistency as you continue to investigate the potential of self-expression. Being aware of who you are is a continuous process that calls for intentionality. Make a commitment to consistently expressing oneself, whether it is via conversations, artistic pursuits, or just talking to loved ones. The conviction that your voice counts and should be heard is strengthened by this regular exercise.

Over time, self-expression might also change. Your perception of who you are will evolve along with you. Accept this flexibility and give yourself permission to experiment with different facets of your own expression. It's quite normal for what speaks to you now to change tomorrow. Being able to express yourself freely can enhance your identity and help you develop a closer bond with your changing self.

In the end, self-awareness, creativity, and vulnerability come together to form the art of identity ownership. You start a life-changing path of authenticity when you embrace every aspect of who you are and share it with the world. Every act of self-expression serves as a proclamation of your value and uniqueness, acting as a constant reminder that you deserve acceptance and love for who you are.

Managing the intricacies of identity and self-expression is a journey of learning, development, and camaraderie. Celebrate your voice and the distinctive contributions you make to the world as you proceed along this road. Unapologetically embracing who you are empowers not just you but also everyone around you, creating an authentic and accepting culture that extends well beyond your own experiences.

Chapter 2
Embracing Your Uniqueness

Breaking Free from Comparison Culture

It's very simple to slip into the comparison trap in a world full with well chosen photos, highlight reels, and information that never stops flowing. As we browse social media, we see other people's accomplishments, attractiveness, and seemingly ideal lifestyles, which frequently makes us feel inadequate and self-conscious. This widespread culture of comparison can make it difficult for us to recognize and value our individuality, which weakens our ability to truly appreciate ourselves.

Understanding the negative consequences of comparison is the first step towards accepting your individuality. It frequently causes us to gauge our value based on the achievements or outward looks of others, which feeds a mindset that lives on criticism and condemnation. The voice of self-acceptance may be muffled by a harsh and merciless internal debate brought on by this cycle. We must develop an understanding of our inherent worth and learn to cherish the uniqueness that makes us unique if we are to escape this cycle.

One of the most effective tools in this process is self-awareness. It entails a thorough investigation of your ideas, emotions, and self-perception. Think about the things that make you feel compelled to compare. Are these feelings evoked by particular individuals, events, or platforms? In this sense, journaling may be a beneficial activity. By putting your ideas and emotions on paper, you make room to look at any patterns that show up. Through introspection, you may pinpoint the underlying reasons for your comparisons and get insight into how they impact your sense of self.

It is as crucial to comprehend the social variables that drive comparison. Many of us are socialized to compete for approval from an early age, whether it is through social standing, academic success, or physical attractiveness. These outside norms have the power to distort how we perceive contentment and success. You may reinterpret what success means to you individually by realizing that these measurements are frequently arbitrary. It opens the door to a greater understanding of your individual path by moving the emphasis from outside approval to inner fulfillment.

Questioning the stories we tell ourselves is another way to escape comparison culture. Negative self-talk is frequently sustained by the internal critic, who frequently lives on comparisons. Remind yourself of your successes and talents whenever you catch yourself comparing yourself to others. Understand that every person's path is different and that what suits one person might not suit you. You may develop an attitude of thankfulness for your own experiences and attributes by changing your perspective from one of competition to one of joy.

Another essential component of accepting your individuality is discovering your tribe. An atmosphere where self-acceptance may flourish is created by surrounding yourself with people who value you for who you are. You may express yourself freely in these connections without worrying about being judged. Your resolve to embrace your uniqueness can be strengthened by participating in conversations that value honesty and variety.

Taking use of your individuality is crucial. Why are you who you are? Investigating your values, interests, and passions may provide valuable information, even if this inquiry may appear straightforward. Accept the things that make you happy and curious. Engaging with your distinctive qualities, whether they be a passion, skill, or philosophy, enables you to develop a closer bond with yourself. Honor these qualities without evaluating them against others; keep in mind that your emotions and interests are legitimate regardless of how they compare to social norms.

One important factor in escaping comparison is mindfulness. You can concentrate on your own experiences without being sidetracked by outside standards when you are in the present. You may focus your thoughts and lessen feelings of inadequacy by engaging in practices like yoga, meditation, or just spending time in nature. You develop a respect for your individual journey when you practice mindfulness, which makes you more aware of your own emotions and desires.

Accepting your imperfections is another essential component of appreciating your individuality. It's simple to believe that we have to project a faultless picture to the outside world in a society that frequently exalts perfectionism. However, you may free yourself from unattainable ideals by accepting that imperfection is a normal aspect of the human experience. Accept your peculiarities and imperfections as essential components of who you are. They provide depth to your narrative and help you come across as genuine and relatable. In addition to improving your self-love, this acceptance inspires others to accept their flaws.

In the current digital era, cultivating a positive connection with social media is crucial. Social media sites may be motivating, but they can also make people feel more like they're being compared to others. Make sure that the accounts you have on the internet support diversity, positivism, and genuineness. Those that make you feel inadequate or self-conscious should be unfollowed or muted. You may foster a more encouraging atmosphere that strengthens your resolve to embrace your individuality by deliberately selecting the material you take in.

Gratitude exercises are another powerful tactic. You may change your perspective from what you lack to what you have by routinely recognizing the things in your life that you value. By fostering an attitude of plenty, this practice strengthens the notion that your path is worthwhile and legitimate. Think considering starting a thankfulness diary in which you record your accomplishments, your favorite aspects of yourself, and the special moments that have influenced your life. This activity is a potent reminder of your inherent value and uniqueness.

Furthermore, it's frequently necessary to push yourself beyond your comfort zone in order to embrace your individuality. You may uncover your secret passions and skills by pushing yourself and trying new things. Every new endeavor offers a chance to discover more about oneself, whether it's attending a class, visiting a new location, or giving a speech in front of an audience. These encounters can boost your self-esteem and solidify your sense of your individuality.

It is impossible to overestimate the importance of self-expression on this journey. It may be very freeing to find methods to express your ideas, emotions, and experiences. You may discover and celebrate your uniqueness via self-expression, whether it be through writing, painting, music, or other creative endeavors. In addition to increasing self-awareness, this process gives your distinct individuality a physical manifestation. By sharing your artistic pursuits, you may encourage others to value their individuality and build a community of self-acceptance and authenticity.

Remember that it's acceptable to ask for help while you work through the challenges of accepting your individuality. Attending therapy or counseling can offer a secure setting for thoroughly examining your emotions and experiences. A specialist may assist you in identifying the causes of your comparison inclinations and in creating countermeasures. As you strive to embrace your true self and develop a good self-image, this support may be really helpful.

Self-acceptance and self-discovery are not always easy processes. Moments of insecurity and self-doubt may arise, particularly when you have to face deeply rooted comparison tendencies. But during this process, it's crucial to have patience with oneself. Accepting your individuality is a lifetime process that calls for constant introspection, adaptation, and development. Give yourself permission to enjoy this trip without passing judgment and to acknowledge and appreciate every tiny step you take in the direction of self-acceptance.

Furthermore, understanding how comparison culture affects our relationships might help us develop stronger bonds with others. Seek to establish connections that promote cooperation and support rather than rivalry. Honor one another's accomplishments and support one another when things are tough. You may foster an atmosphere where originality flourishes by cultivating a community based on respect and regard for one another.

It is also uplifting to participate in the larger discussion about accepting oneself and one's individuality. A culture of authenticity that defies social standards may be fostered by sharing your experiences and views with others. Starting conversations on the value of accepting uniqueness might encourage those in your vicinity to consider their own paths. You have a significant impact on changing the conversation on comparison and self-worth by adding your voice to this discussion.

In the end, embracing your individuality is about taking back control of your life. It's an affirmation that who you are is real, admirable, and worthy of celebration. You may fully live your own life by releasing yourself from the constraints of comparison. This newfound independence strengthens the idea that you are sufficient exactly the way you are by enabling you to confidently embrace your true self.

Remember that accepting your individuality is an act of self-love as you proceed down this road. It's a dedication to respecting your uniqueness and appreciating the characteristics that define you. You enable yourself to live life without apology with every step you take in the direction of self-acceptance, encouraging others to follow suit. Your distinct voice is a gift that should be appreciated and acknowledged in a society that frequently places a higher value on comparison.

Celebrating Your Differences

In a world often fixated on ideals of conformity and sameness, embracing and celebrating our differences can feel like an act of defiance. Each of us carries a unique blend of experiences, perspectives, and qualities that shape our identities. Recognizing and valuing these differences not only enriches our lives but also enhances our ability to connect with others. The journey toward embracing your uniqueness is about stepping into your authentic self and recognizing that your distinct qualities are what make you truly special.

At the core of embracing your uniqueness lies self-acceptance. This involves acknowledging every facet of your identity, from your quirks to your strengths. Self-acceptance is not merely about recognizing who you are; it's about appreciating the entirety of your being, including the aspects that society might deem unconventional. This acceptance allows you to let go of the pressure to conform and opens the door to a more genuine expression of self.

A significant aspect of this journey is understanding the narratives we carry. Many of us internalize messages from our upbringing, culture, and society that dictate what is considered "normal" or "acceptable." These narratives can create barriers that inhibit our self-acceptance and self-love. To truly celebrate your differences, it is essential to deconstruct these narratives and question their validity. Ask yourself: Whose voice is speaking when I feel inadequate? Recognizing that these are often external expectations can help liberate you from their constraints.

Cultivating a mindset of curiosity can also be instrumental in embracing your uniqueness. Instead of approaching your differences with apprehension or self-doubt, try to view them as fascinating aspects of your identity to explore. This mindset encourages self-discovery and allows you to engage with your unique traits in a positive light. Consider what makes you different: your interests, your experiences, or even your way of thinking. Approach these differences with an open heart and mind, and you may uncover hidden strengths and insights.

One of the most empowering ways to celebrate your uniqueness is through self-expression. Engaging in creative activities—whether it's writing, painting, dancing, or any form of art—allows you to communicate your individuality in a tangible way. Creative expression serves as a powerful outlet for emotions and thoughts, enabling you to share your story with the world. The act of creating is not about perfection; it's about authenticity. Allow yourself to create freely, without the constraints of comparison or judgment. This process can be incredibly liberating, reinforcing the idea that your voice matters.

Surrounding yourself with a supportive community is also vital in this journey. Engaging with people who appreciate and celebrate your uniqueness can have a profound impact on your self-acceptance. Seek out individuals who uplift you and encourage you to express your true self. These relationships can foster an environment of understanding and empathy, allowing you to explore your identity without fear. Authentic connections remind you that you are not alone in your journey; there are others who share similar struggles and triumphs.

In addition to nurturing supportive relationships, it's essential to practice gratitude for your unique qualities. Taking the time to reflect on what you appreciate about yourself can shift your focus from comparison to self-acceptance. Consider keeping a gratitude journal specifically dedicated to acknowledging your individuality. List the traits, experiences, and accomplishments that make you who you are. This practice reinforces the idea that your uniqueness is valuable and deserving of recognition.

Embracing your differences also involves confronting societal expectations that can often feel limiting. From beauty standards to career paths, society tends to promote a narrow definition of success and worth. It's crucial to challenge these norms and redefine what success means for you. Understand that your path may not look like anyone else's, and that's perfectly okay. The richness of life lies in its diversity, and your journey is a vital part of that tapestry. By forging your own path, you inspire others to do the same, fostering a culture that values authenticity over conformity.

As you celebrate your differences, consider the importance of vulnerability. Sharing your authentic self requires courage, particularly in a world that often promotes a polished facade. Embracing vulnerability allows you to connect more deeply with others, creating an environment where differences can be acknowledged and celebrated. When you share your struggles and triumphs, you invite others to do the same, fostering a culture of acceptance and understanding. Vulnerability can be a powerful catalyst for connection, reminding us that we all have unique stories to share.

The power of storytelling is another essential aspect of embracing your uniqueness. Each of us has a narrative shaped by our experiences, and sharing that story can illuminate the beauty of individuality. Consider writing down your journey—what challenges have you faced, and how have they shaped your perspective? When you share your story, you not only honor your experiences but also create opportunities for others to reflect on their own journeys. Storytelling fosters connection and empathy, reminding us that our differences are not barriers but bridges that unite us.

Engaging with your cultural and personal heritage can also deepen your appreciation for your uniqueness. Exploring your background—whether through traditions, family stories, or cultural practices—can enhance your understanding of yourself and your place in the world. Celebrate the richness of your heritage and how it contributes to your identity. This exploration can serve as a reminder that your differences are not something to hide but rather something to embrace and showcase.

In the pursuit of embracing your uniqueness, it's important to practice self-compassion. Acknowledge that the journey toward self-acceptance may have its ups and downs. There may be moments of doubt or insecurity, and that's entirely normal. When these feelings arise, treat yourself with the same kindness you would offer a friend. Understand that self-acceptance is a process that requires patience and gentleness. By nurturing a compassionate relationship with yourself, you create a solid foundation for celebrating your differences.

Additionally, stepping outside of your comfort zone can lead to profound discoveries about your uniqueness. Trying new experiences, meeting new people, and exploring different environments can challenge your perspectives and encourage personal growth. Each new venture provides an opportunity to learn more about yourself and what makes you tick. Embrace these moments of exploration as valuable insights into your identity, and allow them to inform your journey of self-acceptance.

Engaging with the broader conversation about diversity and inclusion can also empower your journey. By actively participating in discussions about the importance of embracing differences, you contribute to a culture that values individuality. Your voice can inspire others to reflect on their own identities and challenge societal norms that perpetuate comparison. Engaging with communities that celebrate diversity reinforces the notion that our differences enrich the human experience.

Moreover, practicing mindfulness can enhance your ability to embrace your uniqueness. Mindfulness encourages you to be present in the moment, allowing you to fully experience your thoughts and feelings without judgment. When you cultivate a mindful approach, you become more attuned to your own needs and desires, making it easier to appreciate what makes you unique. Mindfulness can help quiet the noise of comparison, enabling you to focus on your journey rather than the paths of others.

As you navigate the complexities of embracing your differences, consider the role of self-care. Prioritizing your well-being is essential in nurturing your individuality. Engage in activities that recharge and nourish you, whether it's spending time in nature, practicing yoga, or indulging in creative pursuits. By caring for yourself, you reinforce the idea that your uniqueness is worthy of attention and appreciation. Self-care acts as a reminder that your journey is valuable and deserving of investment.

In the process of celebrating your uniqueness, remember to challenge the comparisons that may arise. When you find yourself measuring your worth against others, pause and reflect on the value of your own experiences. Engage in affirmations that reinforce your individuality and remind you of your strengths. Shift your focus from competition to collaboration, recognizing that each person's journey is valid and deserving of celebration.

Ultimately, embracing your uniqueness is a transformative journey that fosters self-love and acceptance. By recognizing the beauty in your differences, you cultivate a sense of pride in your identity. This journey allows you to navigate life unapologetically, celebrating the qualities that make you who you are. In a world that often encourages conformity, your uniqueness is a powerful statement of authenticity, inspiring others to embrace their individuality as well. As you continue on this path, remember that your differences are not only worth celebrating but are also essential to the rich tapestry of human experience.

Chapter 3
From Self-Doubt to Self-Worth

Overcoming the Fear of Judgment

Navigating the landscape of self-worth often involves confronting the deep-seated fear of judgment. This fear can manifest in various forms—hesitation to express oneself, reluctance to pursue dreams, or the tendency to seek validation from others. Understanding and overcoming this fear is crucial in the journey toward embracing your authentic self and cultivating a profound sense of self-worth.

Self-doubt is a pervasive emotion that can infiltrate many aspects of our lives. It often begins with a critical internal dialogue, one that may echo the negative messages we've received throughout our lives. Whether through societal standards, familial expectations, or past experiences, this internal critic can become a formidable force, whispering that we are not enough. Recognizing this voice is the first step in dismantling its power. By becoming aware of the narratives that fuel your self-doubt, you can begin to challenge and reframe them.

The process of overcoming self-doubt starts with self-awareness. Spend time reflecting on the origins of your doubts. What triggers these feelings? Are there specific situations, people, or experiences that exacerbate your insecurities? Journaling can be an effective tool for this exploration. By writing down your thoughts and feelings, you create a space for introspection. This practice allows you to trace the roots of your self-doubt, helping you understand its influence on your life.

Once you identify the sources of your self-doubt, consider how these narratives have shaped your self-image. Many of us internalize messages from childhood or adolescence that inform our beliefs about ourselves. Perhaps a teacher dismissed your talents, or a peer's comment made you question your abilities. Acknowledging these experiences can help you recontextualize them. They are not definitive reflections of your worth but rather experiences that do not define who you are.

Challenging negative beliefs requires a conscious effort to replace them with affirming thoughts. This process often involves creating a list of positive affirmations that resonate with you. These affirmations should reflect your values, strengths, and aspirations. For example, phrases like "I am enough," "I am deserving of love and respect," or "My voice matters" can serve as powerful reminders of your inherent worth. Repeat these affirmations daily, particularly in moments of doubt. Over time, they can help shift your mindset from one of self-criticism to self-acceptance.

Another key aspect of overcoming the fear of judgment is reframing how you perceive criticism. Instead of viewing judgment as a reflection of your worth, consider it an opportunity for growth. Every piece of feedback—whether positive or negative—can provide valuable insights. Embracing a growth mindset allows you to see challenges as stepping stones toward improvement rather than insurmountable obstacles. This shift in perspective can significantly reduce the power that judgment holds over you.

Engaging in self-compassion is also essential in this journey. Rather than berating yourself for perceived shortcomings, treat yourself with the same kindness you would offer a friend. When self-doubt creeps in, pause and acknowledge your feelings without judgment. Understand that everyone experiences doubt and insecurity at times. Embracing this commonality can foster a sense of connection with others and remind you that you are not alone in your struggles.

Surrounding yourself with supportive individuals is crucial in cultivating self-worth. Seek out friends, mentors, and communities that uplift and encourage you. These relationships can serve as a protective buffer against the fear of judgment. When you are surrounded by people who celebrate your uniqueness and value your contributions, it becomes easier to dismiss negative self-talk. Engage in open conversations with these individuals about your fears and insecurities. Often, sharing your vulnerabilities can strengthen connections and foster mutual support.

Another powerful tool in overcoming self-doubt is the practice of vulnerability. Allowing yourself to be vulnerable can feel daunting, especially when the fear of judgment looms large. However, vulnerability is a crucial element of authenticity. When you share your true self—your dreams, fears, and struggles—you invite deeper connections with others. This openness can create an environment where judgment is replaced with understanding and empathy. By embracing vulnerability, you assert your worthiness and establish a foundation for genuine relationships.

Additionally, stepping outside of your comfort zone can be transformative in building self-worth. When you confront situations that provoke fear, you create opportunities for growth and empowerment. Start small—set achievable goals that push you slightly beyond your comfort zone. Each successful experience can bolster your confidence and challenge the narratives of self-doubt. As you accumulate these victories, you begin to rewrite the story of your capabilities and worth.

Practicing mindfulness can further aid in overcoming the fear of judgment. Mindfulness encourages you to stay present in the moment, reducing the tendency to ruminate on past experiences or worry about future evaluations. When you practice mindfulness, you cultivate awareness of your thoughts and feelings without judgment. This practice helps you observe self-critical thoughts as they arise, allowing you to acknowledge them without being consumed by them. Techniques such as meditation, deep breathing, or grounding exercises can foster a sense of calm and clarity, empowering you to respond to challenges with resilience.

Engaging in activities that ignite your passions can also reinforce your self-worth. Pursuing hobbies and interests that bring you joy allows you to express yourself authentically. When you immerse yourself in what you love, you create a sense of fulfillment that is independent of external validation. This intrinsic motivation serves as a reminder that your worth is not contingent upon others' opinions. Celebrate your passions and embrace the uniqueness they bring to your identity.

As you navigate the complexities of overcoming self-doubt, remember the importance of celebrating your achievements—no matter how small. Recognize your accomplishments and take time to reflect on the progress you've made. Keep a journal of your successes, both big and small, and revisit it regularly. This practice reinforces the idea that you are worthy of celebration and acknowledgment. It also provides a tangible reminder of your growth, helping to counteract moments of self-doubt.

Engaging with the larger community can provide further support in overcoming the fear of judgment. Seek out groups or organizations that resonate with your values and interests. Being part of a community that champions authenticity can bolster your confidence and reinforce the belief that your voice matters. Sharing your experiences with like-minded individuals can help normalize feelings of self-doubt and create a safe space for open dialogue.

Additionally, consider the impact of the media you consume on your self-perception. The narratives and images portrayed in popular culture can heavily influence our beliefs about ourselves. Be mindful of the content you engage with—seek out media that promotes diversity, inclusivity, and authentic representations of self-worth. Curating your media landscape can create a more positive environment that encourages self-acceptance and celebration of individuality.

Overcoming the fear of judgment often requires setting healthy boundaries. Learn to recognize situations or individuals that consistently trigger self-doubt or judgment. Establishing boundaries allows you to protect your emotional well-being and create space for positive influences. It's okay to distance yourself from relationships or environments that undermine your self-worth. By prioritizing your mental health, you affirm your value and reinforce the importance of self-love.

As you work through self-doubt, consider the power of gratitude. Cultivating a gratitude practice can shift your focus from what you perceive as lacking to the abundance in your life. Take time each day to reflect on the things you appreciate about yourself and your experiences. This practice fosters a sense of contentment and reinforces the belief that you are deserving of love and respect. Gratitude can serve as a powerful antidote to self-doubt, reminding you of the positive aspects of your identity.

In this journey, it's vital to acknowledge that overcoming self-doubt is a gradual process. There will be moments of struggle, but it's essential to be patient and compassionate with yourself. Recognize that setbacks are a natural part of growth. Instead of viewing these moments as failures, frame them as opportunities for learning and resilience. Each experience contributes to your journey toward self-worth and authenticity.

Lastly, remember that the fear of judgment will likely always be present to some degree. The goal is not to eliminate this fear entirely but to learn how to navigate it with confidence. Embrace the idea that judgment is often a reflection of others' insecurities rather than a commentary on your worth. By shifting your focus from external validation to internal acceptance, you can cultivate a more profound sense of self-worth that withstands the challenges of judgment.

The journey from self-doubt to self-worth is a powerful testament to the resilience of the human spirit. By confronting the fear of judgment and embracing your authentic self, you pave the way for a life filled with self-acceptance, love, and empowerment. This journey allows you to step into your true potential, inspiring others to do the same. Embracing who you are unapologetically is a declaration of your worthiness, and it creates a ripple effect that encourages others to celebrate their own unique identities. As you continue on this path, remember that you are worthy of love, respect, and belonging, just as you are.

Building Confidence from Within

The journey from self-doubt to self-worth is one that many people embark on, often feeling overwhelmed by the pressures of societal expectations and internal critics. Building confidence from within requires intentional effort and a deep commitment to understanding oneself. It involves peeling back the layers of doubt that can cloud our perception of who we are and what we are capable of achieving.

Self-doubt often stems from various sources, including past experiences, societal conditioning, and comparisons with others. It's a pervasive feeling that can seep into every aspect of life, from personal relationships to professional aspirations. To shift this narrative, one must first cultivate self-awareness. Understanding where your self-doubt originates is crucial in dismantling its grip. Take the time to reflect on your past experiences. Were there specific events or interactions that led to feelings of inadequacy? By identifying these moments, you can begin to reframe them, understanding that they do not define your worth.

This journey of self-discovery may also involve confronting societal pressures that dictate what success or beauty looks like. Many of us have grown up with ideals that are unrealistic and often unattainable. Recognizing that these standards are social constructs can help liberate you from their constraints. Your worth is not determined by how closely you align with these ideals but rather by the unique qualities and strengths that you possess. Embracing your individuality is a powerful step toward building lasting confidence.

Engaging in positive self-talk is another essential element of fostering self-worth. The internal dialogue we maintain significantly impacts our self-image. When self-doubt arises, it often comes accompanied by a harsh inner critic. Challenge this negativity by actively replacing it with affirmations that highlight your strengths and accomplishments. Simple statements like "I am capable," "I deserve love and respect," or "I am enough" can shift your mindset over time. Repeating these affirmations regularly reinforces a more positive self-perception and lays the foundation for genuine confidence.

It's also vital to celebrate your achievements, no matter how small. Often, we focus on what we haven't done or what we perceive as failures. This mindset can obscure our sense of accomplishment. Create a habit of acknowledging your successes, whether they are personal milestones, professional achievements, or acts of kindness. Keeping a journal dedicated to your accomplishments can serve as a tangible reminder of your capabilities. By reflecting on these moments, you reinforce the belief that you are deserving of self-worth.

Building confidence involves taking risks and stepping outside of your comfort zone. While this can be intimidating, pushing yourself to try new experiences fosters growth. Start with small steps—perhaps joining a new class, speaking up in a meeting, or engaging in a hobby you've always been curious about. Each time you step outside your comfort zone, you are challenging the limitations imposed by self-doubt. Over time, these small victories accumulate, boosting your self-esteem and reinforcing the belief that you can handle challenges.

Mindfulness practices can also play a significant role in developing inner confidence. Mindfulness encourages you to stay present and observe your thoughts without judgment. This awareness allows you to recognize self-critical thoughts and detach from them. When you practice mindfulness, you create space to reflect on your feelings, helping to reduce anxiety and self-doubt. Techniques such as meditation, deep breathing, or mindful movement can ground you in the present moment, promoting a sense of calm and clarity.

In addition to mindfulness, self-compassion is crucial for nurturing self-worth. Many people are their harshest critics, often holding themselves to impossibly high standards. Practice treating yourself with kindness, especially in moments of failure or disappointment. Acknowledge that everyone makes mistakes and that these experiences do not diminish your value. Embracing self-compassion allows you to respond to challenges with understanding rather than self-judgment, paving the way for resilience and growth.

Surrounding yourself with positive influences is also an important aspect of building confidence. The people you engage with can significantly impact your self-perception. Seek out individuals who uplift and inspire you—those who encourage you to embrace your unique qualities and celebrate your successes. Constructive relationships create a supportive environment where you can express yourself freely. Engage in conversations that reinforce your worth and remind you of your strengths.

Vulnerability is another powerful tool in the journey to self-worth. Opening up about your fears and insecurities can feel uncomfortable, yet it can also lead to profound connections with others. Sharing your experiences fosters empathy and understanding, reminding you that you are not alone in your struggles. When you embrace vulnerability, you demonstrate courage and authenticity, both of which contribute to building confidence from within.

In pursuing self-worth, it is essential to establish boundaries that protect your emotional well-being. Identify situations or individuals that drain your energy or contribute to feelings of self-doubt. Setting boundaries allows you to prioritize your mental health and create a safe space for self-acceptance. By advocating for your needs, you assert your value and reinforce the idea that you are deserving of respect.

Engaging in activities that ignite your passions is also instrumental in building self-confidence. When you pursue what brings you joy, you tap into your authentic self. Whether it's painting, writing, dancing, or volunteering, immersing yourself in your passions fosters a sense of fulfillment. This intrinsic motivation serves as a reminder that your worth is not dependent on external validation but rather on the joy and fulfillment you derive from your interests.

Another critical component of fostering self-worth is learning to accept and embrace imperfection. Society often perpetuates the notion that perfection is the ultimate goal, leading many to feel inadequate. Understand that imperfections are part of the human experience. They add depth to your character and make you relatable. Embracing imperfection allows you to let go of the pressure to conform to unrealistic standards and accept yourself as you are.

Practicing gratitude can also be a transformative aspect of building self-worth. Reflecting on the aspects of your life that you appreciate can shift your focus from what you perceive as lacking to the abundance that exists. Consider keeping a gratitude journal, where you note the things you are thankful for, including your unique qualities and experiences. This practice fosters a mindset of abundance, reinforcing the belief that you are deserving of love and respect.

Engaging in self-reflection can provide valuable insights into your journey toward self-worth. Set aside time to evaluate your thoughts, feelings, and behaviors. What patterns emerge? Are there recurring themes that contribute to your self-doubt? This reflective practice encourages you to take ownership of your narrative, empowering you to make conscious choices that align with your values and aspirations.

Finding a mentor or coach can also be a beneficial step in building confidence. A mentor can offer guidance, encouragement, and valuable perspectives on your journey. They can help you identify your strengths and provide constructive feedback. This support can serve as a powerful reminder that you are not alone in your quest for self-worth. Engaging with someone who believes in your potential can inspire you to embrace your capabilities fully.

In the pursuit of self-worth, it's important to embrace a growth mindset. This perspective emphasizes that abilities and intelligence can be developed through dedication and hard work. Embracing challenges, persisting through setbacks, and learning from criticism all contribute to personal growth. When you adopt a growth mindset, you shift your focus from fear of failure to the excitement of learning. This shift can significantly enhance your confidence and resilience.

As you work on building self-worth, remember that progress is not always linear. There will be days when self-doubt resurfaces, and that's perfectly normal. Instead of becoming discouraged, acknowledge these feelings and remind yourself of the tools you have at your disposal. Lean into your support system, practice self-compassion, and return to your affirmations. Building confidence is a continuous journey, one that requires patience and perseverance.

Engaging in physical activities can also contribute to your sense of self-worth. Exercise releases endorphins, which enhance mood and overall well-being. Whether it's going for a walk, joining a fitness class, or practicing yoga, physical movement allows you to connect with your body and cultivate a sense of empowerment. This connection can reinforce positive self-image and promote feelings of strength and vitality.

Additionally, exploring new interests or hobbies can provide a fresh perspective on your abilities. Trying something new can be exhilarating and daunting, but it often leads to personal growth. Embrace the opportunity to learn and expand your skill set. Whether it's picking up an instrument, learning a new language, or taking up a sport, each new experience enhances your confidence and showcases your willingness to step outside your comfort zone.

Developing emotional intelligence is also essential in building self-worth. Understanding your emotions and how they impact your thoughts and behaviors enables you to navigate challenges more effectively. This awareness fosters resilience and empowers you to respond to self-doubt with clarity and intention. Consider practices such as journaling or seeking therapy to explore your emotional landscape further. These tools can provide valuable insights into your journey toward self-acceptance.

Connecting with your values and purpose can also enhance your self-worth. Reflect on what truly matters to you—what are your core beliefs and aspirations? When you align your actions with your values, you cultivate a sense of authenticity that reinforces your worth. Engaging in meaningful activities that resonate with your purpose creates a profound sense of fulfillment and self-acceptance.

The journey from self-doubt to self-worth is ultimately about embracing your authentic self. Each step you take toward understanding and valuing your unique qualities strengthens your confidence from within. By challenging negative narratives, surrounding yourself with positivity, and engaging in practices that nurture self-love, you pave the way for a more fulfilling and empowered life.

As you continue on this path, remember that self-worth is an ongoing journey. Celebrate the progress you make and acknowledge the challenges you overcome. By prioritizing your growth and embracing your individuality, you inspire others to embark on their own journeys toward self-acceptance. Embracing who you are, flaws and all, is a powerful declaration of your worthiness. Trust in your potential, and allow yourself to thrive unapologetically.

Chapter 4
Authenticity in Relationships

Setting Boundaries with Grace

Authenticity in relationships is a vital aspect of fostering genuine connections with others. It involves being true to yourself while navigating the complexities of interpersonal dynamics. At the heart of authenticity lies the ability to communicate your needs, desires, and limitations effectively. This is where the art of setting boundaries comes into play—a necessary skill for maintaining healthy relationships and ensuring mutual respect.

Understanding what boundaries are is crucial. They are not walls meant to keep people out but rather guidelines that establish what is acceptable and what is not. Boundaries help define your personal space, allowing you to honor your feelings and needs without compromising your values. When boundaries are clear, relationships can thrive on trust, understanding, and support.

Establishing boundaries often requires introspection. Take time to reflect on your values, priorities, and emotional needs. What are the areas in your life where you feel your boundaries may be blurred or overlooked? Are there specific situations or interactions that leave you feeling drained or uncomfortable? By identifying these patterns, you can begin to articulate your needs more clearly, setting the stage for healthier interactions.

Communication is a key component of boundary-setting. It is essential to express your boundaries in a way that is direct yet respectful. When you communicate your needs, focus on "I" statements rather than "you" statements. For example, instead of saying, "You always interrupt me," try framing it as, "I feel unheard when conversations are interrupted." This approach helps to convey your feelings without placing blame, making it easier for others to understand your perspective.

Clarity is vital when discussing your boundaries. Be specific about what is acceptable and what is not. This clarity helps eliminate ambiguity, reducing the likelihood of misunderstandings. Whether in personal relationships or professional settings, being upfront about your expectations creates a foundation of mutual respect. Remember that setting boundaries is not about being rigid; it's about creating a framework that supports your emotional well-being.

Establishing boundaries can sometimes evoke feelings of guilt, especially if you have been conditioned to prioritize others' needs over your own. It's important to recognize that setting boundaries is not selfish; it is an act of self-care. When you prioritize your needs, you create a healthier dynamic that ultimately benefits everyone involved. Remember, you cannot pour from an empty cup. By taking care of yourself first, you are better equipped to support others.

In relationships, it's crucial to recognize that boundaries can be fluid. They may change over time based on your evolving needs and circumstances. Being open to re-evaluating your boundaries encourages ongoing communication and understanding. If you find that a boundary you set no longer serves you, don't hesitate to express this. Engaging in open dialogues about boundary adjustments demonstrates vulnerability and fosters deeper connections.

When setting boundaries, it's essential to anticipate potential reactions. Not everyone will respond positively to your newfound assertiveness. Some may feel challenged or threatened, particularly if they are accustomed to a different dynamic. Approaching these conversations with empathy can ease tension. Acknowledge the other person's feelings while remaining firm in your stance. You can express, "I understand this might be difficult for you, but this is what I need for my well-being."

Additionally, consistency is key. Once you establish boundaries, it's essential to uphold them. Inconsistency can lead to confusion and resentment, undermining the trust you are trying to build. If you find yourself bending your boundaries to please others, take a moment to reassess your motivations. Are you seeking validation or approval? Recognizing these patterns allows you to reinforce your boundaries with confidence.

As you navigate boundary-setting, self-compassion plays an important role. Be gentle with yourself throughout this process. There will be moments of discomfort and uncertainty as you learn to assert your needs. Acknowledge that it is normal to feel anxious about setting boundaries, especially if it challenges the status quo. Practicing self-compassion helps to alleviate this anxiety, allowing you to approach difficult conversations with grace.

It's also beneficial to practice active listening in your relationships. When discussing boundaries, give the other person an opportunity to share their thoughts and feelings. Listening attentively fosters a sense of collaboration and respect. It signals that you value their perspective, even if it differs from your own. By creating a safe space for dialogue, you encourage a more profound understanding of each other's needs.

In some cases, you may encounter individuals who struggle to respect your boundaries, regardless of how clearly you communicate them. It's essential to recognize that you cannot control others' reactions, but you can control how you respond. If someone consistently disregards your boundaries, it may be necessary to reassess the relationship. Healthy relationships are built on mutual respect, and if that respect is absent, it may be time to reevaluate your involvement.

Embracing authenticity means being true to yourself while allowing others to be themselves as well. It involves accepting that not everyone will respond positively to your boundaries, and that's okay. Authentic relationships thrive on the understanding that individuals can coexist while honoring their differences. This acceptance creates an environment where everyone feels empowered to express their needs.

When you establish boundaries with grace, you also model this behavior for others. By demonstrating that it is okay to prioritize one's needs, you create a ripple effect, encouraging those around you to do the same. Authenticity fosters a culture of openness, where individuals feel safe to communicate their boundaries and desires. This shared understanding strengthens relationships and enhances emotional intimacy.

Emotional intelligence is a valuable asset in navigating boundary-setting. Being aware of your emotions and the emotions of others allows for a more nuanced approach. Recognize how certain situations impact your feelings and communicate this to those involved. By articulating your emotions, you create a deeper connection and understanding, paving the way for healthy boundaries.

Practicing self-reflection can further enhance your ability to set boundaries. Take time to evaluate your interactions and relationships. Are there recurring patterns that signal the need for boundaries? Reflecting on these dynamics allows you to identify areas for growth. Journaling can be a powerful tool in this process, providing insight into your feelings and reactions over time.

In your pursuit of authenticity, remember that it's okay to seek support. Whether it's a trusted friend, therapist, or coach, having someone to confide in can help you navigate the challenges of boundary-setting. Sharing your experiences with a supportive individual can provide perspective and encouragement, reminding you that you are not alone in this journey.

Boundaries are not merely limitations; they are an expression of your values and self-respect. They communicate to others what you are willing to accept and what you are not. By asserting your boundaries, you demonstrate your commitment to honoring your own needs while creating space for others to do the same. This reciprocity lays the foundation for healthy, authentic relationships.

As you cultivate authenticity in your relationships, be mindful of the impact of external influences. The world often sends messages that prioritize compliance and sacrifice over self-care. Challenge these narratives by reaffirming your right to set boundaries. Trust that honoring your needs does not diminish your capacity to love and support others. In fact, it enhances your ability to engage with them fully and authentically.

Practicing gratitude can also enhance your ability to set boundaries. When you focus on the positive aspects of your relationships, it becomes easier to communicate your needs with love and appreciation. Acknowledge the strengths of your relationships and express gratitude for the support you receive. This positivity creates a more harmonious environment for boundary-setting, allowing for open and constructive conversations.

It's important to understand that setting boundaries is an ongoing process. Your needs may evolve, and so will your relationships. Embrace the fluidity of boundary-setting, recognizing that it's okay to adjust your boundaries as circumstances change. Regularly check in with yourself and those around you to ensure that the established boundaries continue to serve your emotional well-being.

Emphasizing personal responsibility is also crucial in boundary-setting. Each individual has a role in maintaining the balance of a relationship. Recognize that while you can communicate your boundaries, others are responsible for respecting them. This understanding empowers you to assert your needs confidently, fostering a sense of agency in your relationships.

As you navigate the complexities of authenticity and boundary-setting, remember that it's okay to seek feedback from trusted individuals. Engaging in conversations about your boundaries can provide valuable insights and perspectives. Ask for input on how your boundaries impact others and be open to constructive feedback. This dialogue can lead to greater understanding and cooperation in your relationships.

In the realm of authenticity, vulnerability is an essential companion. Embracing vulnerability allows you to connect with others on a deeper level. When you share your authentic self, you invite others to do the same. This exchange fosters trust and intimacy, creating a space where boundaries can be communicated openly and without fear.

In challenging moments, remind yourself of the importance of self-advocacy. Your feelings and needs are valid, and advocating for them is a form of self-respect. Cultivating this mindset empowers you to communicate your boundaries confidently, regardless of the reactions you may encounter. Trust that your voice matters and that your needs deserve to be honored.

As you continue to explore authenticity in your relationships, take time to celebrate your progress. Acknowledge the strides you've made in asserting your boundaries and honoring your needs. Celebrate the relationships that thrive on mutual respect and understanding. Each step you take toward authenticity strengthens your connections and nurtures your sense of self-worth.

Ultimately, authenticity in relationships is about creating a space where everyone feels valued and respected. By setting boundaries with grace, you foster an environment where open communication flourishes. This reciprocity allows for deeper connections and a sense of belonging, reinforcing the idea that you are deserving of love and respect just as you are.

As you embrace your authentic power and practice setting boundaries, trust in your ability to navigate the complexities of relationships with confidence. Remember that your journey is unique, and every step you take toward authenticity is a testament to your commitment to self-love. By honoring your needs and establishing healthy boundaries, you create a life filled with meaningful connections and genuine fulfillment.

Building Honest Connections

Building honest connections in relationships begins with authenticity. To forge meaningful bonds with others, we must first understand and embrace our true selves. Authenticity allows us to show up as we are, without masks or facades, creating a foundation of trust and openness. This genuine presence not only enriches our interactions but also fosters a deeper understanding of ourselves and those around us.

At the core of authenticity lies self-awareness. Understanding who you are—your values, beliefs, and emotions—is essential for building honest connections. Self-reflection plays a crucial role in this process. Take time to explore your feelings, motivations, and desires. What drives you? What are your passions? Engaging in this introspective work enables you to articulate your thoughts and feelings clearly, making it easier to share them with others.

The journey toward authenticity often requires vulnerability. Sharing your true self can be daunting, especially in a world that often values conformity over individuality. Yet, vulnerability is the gateway to genuine connection. When you allow others to see your fears, insecurities, and dreams, you invite them to do the same. This mutual openness fosters a sense of safety and acceptance, creating an environment where honest conversations can thrive.

Communicating authentically means expressing yourself honestly while remaining considerate of others' feelings. It involves sharing your thoughts and feelings without the fear of judgment. When you communicate openly, you encourage those around you to reciprocate. This two-way street of honesty nurtures trust, allowing relationships to deepen and evolve.

Active listening is another key component of building authentic connections. When engaging with others, it's essential to give your full attention. This means not just hearing their words but truly understanding their emotions and perspectives. Ask open-ended questions and reflect on what they share. This practice not only validates their feelings but also reinforces your commitment to an authentic relationship. By demonstrating that you genuinely care, you encourage others to be honest and open in return.

Establishing boundaries is crucial for maintaining authenticity in relationships. Boundaries are not barriers; rather, they define your limits and communicate your needs. By clearly stating what is acceptable and what is not, you create a safe space for both yourself and others. This openness allows for honest conversations about expectations and encourages mutual respect. When both parties feel comfortable expressing their boundaries, the relationship can flourish.

It's also important to recognize that authenticity can sometimes lead to discomfort. Being true to yourself may challenge the status quo in your relationships, especially if others are used to a different dynamic. This can result in resistance or conflict. Approach these situations with empathy. Understand that others may need time to adjust to the changes you are introducing. Be patient and remain steadfast in your commitment to authenticity, as this is often the path to deeper connections.

As you navigate relationships, practicing self-compassion is essential. Recognize that being authentic doesn't mean you have to be perfect. Embrace your flaws and imperfections as part of your unique identity. This acceptance not only enhances your self-esteem but also encourages others to embrace their own vulnerabilities. When you create an environment of self-acceptance, you inspire those around you to share their authentic selves.

Cultivating emotional intelligence can significantly enhance your ability to build honest connections. Emotional intelligence involves recognizing and managing your emotions while understanding and empathizing with the emotions of others. This skill allows for more nuanced conversations and helps you navigate difficult discussions with grace. When you approach interactions with emotional awareness, you create an atmosphere of respect and understanding that fosters authenticity.

Honesty in relationships also means being transparent about your intentions. Clear communication about your desires and expectations helps eliminate misunderstandings. This transparency builds trust and allows both parties to feel secure in their interactions. Share your goals for the relationship and encourage your partner or friend to do the same. By aligning your intentions, you create a shared vision that strengthens your bond.

Conflict is a natural part of any relationship, but how you approach it can either strengthen or weaken your connection. Authenticity during conflicts involves addressing issues head-on rather than avoiding them. When disagreements arise, communicate your feelings openly and constructively. Use "I" statements to express your emotions without placing blame. For example, say, "I feel hurt when..." instead of "You always..." This approach encourages a more honest dialogue and helps prevent defensiveness.

It's essential to recognize the value of forgiveness in authentic relationships. Holding onto grudges or resentment can create emotional barriers, preventing genuine connection. When conflicts arise, focus on understanding rather than winning. Practice empathy and strive to see the situation from the other person's perspective. Acknowledging mistakes, both yours and theirs, allows for healing and growth. This process reinforces the notion that authenticity encompasses not just the good but also the challenging aspects of relationships.

Another vital element of authenticity is celebrating differences. Every individual brings their unique experiences, perspectives, and backgrounds to a relationship. Rather than viewing these differences as obstacles, embrace them as opportunities for growth and learning. Engaging with diverse viewpoints enriches your understanding of the world and fosters deeper connections. Encourage open conversations about these differences, as they often lead to profound insights and shared experiences.

Trust is a fundamental component of authentic relationships. Building trust takes time and consistency. Be reliable and follow through on your commitments. When others see that you honor your word, they are more likely to reciprocate with trust. Trust is reinforced through vulnerability and open communication. The more you share and listen, the stronger the bond becomes.

As you work to cultivate authenticity, it's essential to be aware of external influences that may impact your relationships. Society often imposes expectations and norms that can pressure individuals to conform. Challenge these narratives by reaffirming your right to express your true self. Surround yourself with individuals who value authenticity and encourage you to embrace your uniqueness. This support system serves as a reminder that honest connections are built on genuine acceptance.

Additionally, practicing gratitude can enhance your relationships and foster authenticity. Regularly expressing appreciation for the people in your life strengthens your connections. Acknowledge their contributions and the impact they have on your life. Gratitude cultivates a positive atmosphere, encouraging open communication and deeper engagement. This appreciation reinforces the notion that authentic relationships thrive on mutual support.

In navigating the journey of authenticity, it's crucial to be patient with yourself and others. Developing honest connections takes time and effort. Recognize that not every interaction will go as planned. Some conversations may be challenging or uncomfortable, and that's perfectly normal. Allow yourself and others the grace to learn and grow from these experiences. Embrace the journey, knowing that each step toward authenticity brings you closer to deeper, more fulfilling relationships.

When fostering authenticity, it's essential to remain flexible. As individuals grow and evolve, so do relationships. Be open to change and adapt your approach as necessary. Recognize that authentic connections may shift over time, and that's a natural part of the process. Embracing this fluidity allows for continued growth and understanding.

The practice of authenticity in relationships extends to self-care. Prioritizing your well-being enables you to show up fully for others. Engage in activities that nourish your soul, whether it's spending time in nature, practicing mindfulness, or pursuing your passions. When you take care of yourself, you are better equipped to engage authentically in your relationships. This self-awareness and self-love radiate outward, creating a positive impact on those around you.

Navigating authenticity in relationships also involves recognizing when to let go. Not all connections are meant to last, and that's okay. If a relationship consistently undermines your sense of self or makes you feel unworthy, it may be time to reassess your involvement. Ending a relationship doesn't negate the value of the experiences shared; it's an acknowledgment of your growth and the need to prioritize your well-being.

Additionally, seeking support from others can enhance your journey toward authenticity. Whether through friendships, therapy, or support groups, having a safe space to explore your thoughts and feelings is invaluable. These connections provide encouragement and accountability, reminding you of your worth and the importance of authenticity. Sharing your experiences with those who understand can help you navigate the complexities of relationships with greater ease.

As you strive to build honest connections, be mindful of the power of your words. Language shapes our interactions and influences how we connect with others. Choose your words thoughtfully, ensuring they reflect your genuine feelings and intentions. Clear and compassionate communication fosters understanding and encourages others to do the same.

In moments of doubt or uncertainty, return to your core values. These principles serve as a compass, guiding your interactions and decisions. When faced with challenging situations, ask yourself if your actions align with your values. This alignment fosters authenticity and ensures that your relationships remain grounded in integrity.

When building honest connections, remember that vulnerability can be a catalyst for growth. Share your experiences, fears, and aspirations openly. This honesty invites others to do the same, creating a cycle of trust and connection. Embrace the discomfort that may accompany vulnerability, knowing that it often leads to deeper understanding and intimacy.

In the end, authenticity in relationships is a journey marked by self-discovery, vulnerability, and mutual respect. By prioritizing honesty and open communication, you create a fertile ground for genuine connections to flourish. Embrace your unique self, and invite others to do the same. As you cultivate these honest relationships, you enrich not only your life but also the lives of those around you, creating a tapestry of connection that is both beautiful and fulfilling.

Chapter 5
The Journey of Self-Love

Daily Practices to Cultivate Self-Love

The journey of self-love is a transformative path that invites us to embrace our worthiness, cultivate compassion, and nurture our relationship with ourselves. It's a continuous process, requiring commitment and intentionality. Self-love isn't simply a fleeting emotion; it's a deep-rooted understanding that you are enough just as you are. To embark on this journey, we must explore daily practices that can help us cultivate a profound sense of self-love.

One of the foundational practices for nurturing self-love is the practice of mindfulness. Mindfulness encourages us to be present in the moment, fostering an awareness of our thoughts and feelings without judgment. Taking time each day to engage in mindful moments can significantly shift our relationship with ourselves. Whether through meditation, deep breathing exercises, or simply taking a walk while paying attention to your surroundings, these practices help ground you in the present. By tuning into your body and emotions, you develop a clearer understanding of your needs and desires, reinforcing your self-worth.

Journaling is another powerful tool for self-exploration and self-acceptance. Setting aside a few minutes each day to write can provide clarity and insight into your inner world. Use your journal to express your thoughts, feelings, and aspirations without censorship. This space is for you alone, allowing you to explore your emotions authentically. Consider starting with prompts such as "What do I appreciate about myself today?" or "What are my dreams and desires?" Over time, this practice can help you recognize patterns, celebrate your achievements, and cultivate a deeper sense of self-love.

Affirmations play a crucial role in reshaping negative self-talk and reinforcing positive beliefs about yourself. Incorporating daily affirmations into your routine can be a powerful practice for cultivating self-love. Create a list of affirmations that resonate with you, focusing on your strengths, qualities, and aspirations. Repeat these affirmations each morning or whenever you need a boost. Phrases like "I am worthy of love and happiness" or "I embrace my unique journey" can help shift your mindset over time. This simple act of speaking kindly to yourself lays the groundwork for a more compassionate relationship with yourself.

Gratitude is a transformative practice that can profoundly impact your sense of self. Taking time each day to acknowledge the things you are grateful for cultivates a positive mindset and enhances your overall well-being. Start a gratitude journal where you list three to five things you appreciate about yourself and your life each day. This practice shifts your focus from what's lacking to what you already possess, reinforcing your sense of self-worth. Embracing gratitude helps you recognize the beauty within yourself and the world around you.

Physical self-care is a vital aspect of self-love that often gets overlooked. Taking care of your body is a way of honoring your existence and valuing yourself. Prioritize activities that nourish your body and mind, whether through regular exercise, nutritious meals, or sufficient rest. Engage in movement that brings you joy, whether it's dancing, yoga, or a brisk walk in nature. By cultivating a healthy relationship with your body, you communicate to yourself that you are deserving of care and respect.

Setting healthy boundaries is an essential practice in your self-love journey. Boundaries protect your energy and emotional well-being. Identify areas in your life where you feel overwhelmed or taken for granted. Reflect on how you can communicate your needs effectively, ensuring that you prioritize your own well-being. Saying no to commitments that drain you allows you to say yes to activities that uplift you. When you honor your boundaries, you send a clear message to yourself that your needs matter.

Engaging in creative expression can be a liberating practice for self-love. Whether through art, writing, music, or any other form of creativity, allowing yourself to express your thoughts and feelings fosters self-acceptance. Creativity provides an outlet for exploring your emotions and discovering new aspects of yourself. Set aside time each week to engage in a creative project that excites you. This practice not only nurtures your self-love but also helps you connect with your authentic self.

Forgiveness is a crucial step on the path to self-love. Often, we hold onto past mistakes or regrets, allowing them to hinder our progress. Learning to forgive yourself is essential for moving forward. Reflect on experiences that have caused you pain or shame, and consciously choose to release those feelings. Understand that everyone makes mistakes and that these experiences do not define your worth. Embrace the idea that growth comes from learning, and allow yourself the grace to let go of what no longer serves you.

Building a supportive community is vital for fostering self-love. Surrounding yourself with individuals who uplift and encourage you can profoundly impact your journey. Seek out relationships that inspire growth and authenticity. Engage in conversations that reinforce your sense of self-worth, and be open to receiving support when needed. Authentic connections provide a safe space to explore your vulnerabilities and celebrate your successes. Invest time in nurturing these relationships, as they play a crucial role in your self-love journey.

Practicing self-compassion is a cornerstone of self-love. It involves treating yourself with the same kindness and understanding that you would offer a friend. When faced with challenges or setbacks, pause and reflect on how you would respond to someone you care about. Acknowledge your feelings without judgment, and offer yourself words of encouragement. Self-compassion allows you to embrace imperfections and recognize that being human involves both triumphs and struggles. This practice fosters a sense of connection to yourself, reminding you that you are not alone in your experiences.

Engaging in positive self-talk can shift your internal dialogue and cultivate self-love. Be mindful of the language you use when speaking to yourself. Replace critical or negative thoughts with affirming and compassionate statements. When you catch yourself engaging in self-criticism, pause and reframe those thoughts. Ask yourself, "What would I say to a friend in this situation?" This shift in perspective fosters a more loving relationship with yourself.

Exploring your passions and interests is another vital practice on your self-love journey. Dedicate time to activities that bring you joy and fulfillment.

Whether it's pursuing a hobby, learning a new skill, or volunteering for a cause you care about, engaging in meaningful activities fosters a sense of purpose and self-worth. When you invest in your passions, you reinforce the belief that you deserve to pursue what makes you happy.

Embracing solitude is an often-overlooked aspect of self-love. Taking time for yourself allows you to recharge and connect with your inner self. Whether through quiet reflection, nature walks, or simply enjoying a cup of tea, solitude provides space for self-discovery. Use this time to reflect on your thoughts and feelings without distractions. Embracing solitude fosters a deeper understanding of yourself and reinforces the importance of your own company.

Practicing mindfulness in daily activities can also enhance your journey of self-love. Whether washing dishes, taking a shower, or walking to work, be fully present in these moments. Notice the sensations, sounds, and feelings associated with these activities. By engaging in mindfulness, you cultivate a deeper connection with yourself and your surroundings, reinforcing the idea that every moment is worthy of your attention and appreciation.

Exploring your values is a significant practice for nurturing self-love. Reflect on what truly matters to you—your beliefs, principles, and what you stand for. Understanding your values helps guide your decisions and actions, ensuring they align with your authentic self. When you live in alignment with your values, you cultivate a sense of integrity and self-respect. Regularly revisit your values and make adjustments as necessary, allowing them to serve as a compass on your self-love journey.

Acknowledging your achievements, no matter how small, is a vital practice for cultivating self-love. Often, we rush past our accomplishments, focusing instead on what we haven't achieved. Take time to celebrate your victories, whether they're related to personal growth, career milestones, or overcoming challenges. Create a ritual for acknowledging your achievements, such as a monthly reflection or a visual representation of your progress. This practice reinforces the idea that you are deserving of recognition and gratitude.

Integrating nature into your routine can significantly enhance your sense of self-love. Spending time outdoors allows you to reconnect with the natural world, fostering a sense of peace and grounding. Whether it's a hike, a walk in the park, or simply sitting outside, nature has a way of reminding us of our connection to the universe. Take time to immerse yourself in the beauty around you, allowing it to rejuvenate your spirit and nourish your sense of self.

As you navigate your journey of self-love, remember that it's essential to be patient with yourself. Progress may not always be linear, and that's perfectly normal. Embrace the ups and downs, recognizing that each step contributes to your growth. Allow yourself the grace to stumble and learn, knowing that every experience is an opportunity for self-discovery.

Creating a vision for your self-love journey can provide clarity and motivation. Visualize where you want to be in terms of your relationship with yourself. What do you want to feel? How do you want to show up in your life? Write down your vision and revisit it regularly. This practice serves as a reminder of your commitment to self-love and allows you to track your progress along the way.

Finally, recognize the power of playfulness in cultivating self-love. Allow yourself to engage in activities that bring joy and laughter. Whether it's dancing, playing games, or spending time with loved ones, embracing playfulness nurtures a light-hearted spirit. By infusing your life with joy, you create space for self-acceptance and happiness.

This journey of self-love is not merely about reaching a destination; it's about embracing the process. Each daily practice you incorporate into your routine builds a foundation for a more compassionate relationship with yourself. Through mindfulness, gratitude, self-compassion, and honest connections, you cultivate a profound sense of self-worth. The journey is unique to each individual, but the common thread lies in the commitment to love yourself unapologetically. As you explore these practices, remember that self-love is an ongoing journey, and every step you take is a celebration of your authenticity and your inherent worth.

Healing Past Wounds and Moving Forward

Embarking on the journey of self-love often necessitates confronting past wounds. These experiences, whether they stem from childhood, relationships, or personal failures, can leave lasting imprints on our self-esteem and perception of worth. Healing these wounds is not merely an act of reflection; it is an essential step in cultivating a loving relationship with ourselves. By acknowledging our pain, processing our emotions, and learning from our experiences, we can transform these past injuries into sources of strength.

Understanding the impact of past wounds is the first step in this healing journey. Often, we carry these experiences as burdens, shaping our thoughts, feelings, and behaviors in ways we may not fully realize. Take time to reflect on significant moments in your life that have influenced your self-perception. This could involve writing about your experiences or discussing them with a trusted friend or therapist. By articulating your story, you begin to disentangle your identity from the pain, allowing you to see these experiences as chapters in your life rather than defining elements.

Processing emotions associated with past wounds is crucial for healing. Many of us have been taught to suppress feelings, fearing that vulnerability may expose us to further hurt. However, allowing ourselves to feel deeply can be liberating. Create a safe space to explore your emotions—whether through journaling, art, or quiet contemplation. Permit yourself to experience sadness, anger, or fear without judgment. This emotional honesty is vital for understanding the depth of your wounds and how they have shaped you.

Forgiveness, both of yourself and others, plays a significant role in healing. Many times, we hold onto grudges or feelings of resentment that only serve to weigh us down. Forgiveness does not mean excusing harmful behavior; rather, it is an act of self-liberation. Recognize that holding onto pain often perpetuates suffering. Reflect on what forgiveness means to you. Consider writing a letter to someone who has hurt you, expressing your feelings and ultimately deciding to release the burden. You may choose not to send the letter, but the act of writing can be cathartic and transformative.

In the context of self-love, it's essential to acknowledge the role of self-compassion in healing. Self-compassion invites us to treat ourselves with the same kindness we would offer a friend. When reflecting on past wounds, practice speaking to yourself gently. Acknowledge that everyone faces challenges and makes mistakes. Instead of harsh self-criticism, allow for understanding and grace. This practice fosters resilience and a nurturing attitude toward your own journey.

Identifying and challenging negative beliefs is a fundamental aspect of moving forward. Past experiences often lead to deeply ingrained beliefs about ourselves, such as "I am not enough" or "I don't deserve love." Begin to recognize these thoughts as they arise. Are they rooted in truth, or are they reflections of past hurt? Challenge these beliefs by questioning their validity. Consider evidence that contradicts them. By reframing these narratives, you pave the way for healthier self-perceptions.

Cultivating a supportive environment is essential for your healing journey. Surround yourself with individuals who uplift and encourage you. Share your journey with those who respect your experiences and provide a listening ear. This network can serve as a powerful reminder that you are not alone in your struggles. Engaging with compassionate and understanding people can help you rebuild trust in others and reinforce your self-worth.

Practicing gratitude is a transformative tool for shifting focus from pain to possibility. Each day, take a moment to reflect on what you appreciate in your life, including your strengths and the progress you've made. Keeping a gratitude journal can help you develop a habit of recognizing the positives amid challenges. This practice fosters a sense of abundance and encourages you to celebrate your resilience.

Embracing vulnerability is an integral part of the healing process. Many of us shy away from vulnerability, associating it with weakness. However, vulnerability is a sign of strength and authenticity. By allowing yourself to be open about your struggles and fears, you invite deeper connections with others. This openness can create a supportive community that reinforces your journey of self-love. Engaging in vulnerability encourages empathy and connection, reminding you that everyone has their battles.

Creating a self-care routine that prioritizes your well-being is essential for healing. Self-care goes beyond indulgence; it involves engaging in practices that nourish your mind, body, and soul. Identify activities that rejuvenate you—be it exercise, meditation, reading, or spending time in nature. Carving out time for self-care sends a powerful message to yourself that you are deserving of love and attention. This commitment to your well-being cultivates a positive relationship with yourself and promotes healing.

Engaging in therapy or counseling can provide invaluable support as you navigate the complexities of past wounds. Professional guidance can help you process your emotions and develop strategies for healing. A therapist offers a safe space to explore your experiences without judgment, enabling you to gain insights and tools for moving forward. Therapy can be a catalyst for transformation, helping you uncover deeper layers of self-awareness and self-acceptance.

Setting healthy boundaries is crucial in the journey of self-love. Boundaries protect your emotional space and reinforce your sense of self-worth. Reflect on areas in your life where you feel overextended or compromised. Learn to communicate your needs effectively, allowing you to honor your own well-being. By establishing boundaries, you create a sanctuary for your growth and healing, signaling to yourself that you deserve to prioritize your needs.

Recognizing the importance of the present moment can be a powerful antidote to past wounds. Many of us become entangled in memories that evoke pain or regret, pulling us away from the beauty of now. Practice mindfulness to anchor yourself in the present. Engage in activities that cultivate awareness, such as meditation, yoga, or simply focusing on your breath. This practice allows you to observe your thoughts and emotions without being overwhelmed by them. By grounding yourself in the present, you begin to shift your focus from past wounds to the possibilities of today.

Exploring new interests and passions can be a liberating way to reclaim your identity beyond past pain. Engaging in activities that excite you fosters a sense of joy and fulfillment. Consider trying something you've always wanted to do, whether it's taking a class, joining a club, or starting a creative project. These experiences can help you reconnect with your sense of self and reinforce the idea that you are a dynamic individual capable of growth and change.

Building resilience is an essential aspect of healing. Resilience enables you to navigate life's challenges with strength and grace. Reflect on past experiences where you have overcome adversity. What strengths did you draw upon during those times? By acknowledging your resilience, you empower yourself to face future challenges with confidence. Embrace setbacks as opportunities for growth, reminding yourself that every obstacle is a chance to learn and evolve.

Practicing self-acceptance is a vital component of your journey toward self-love. Embrace the entirety of your being—the strengths, weaknesses, triumphs, and failures. Understand that you are a work in progress, and that's perfectly okay. Instead of striving for perfection, aim for authenticity. Accepting yourself as you are lays the groundwork for genuine self-love. This acceptance fosters a sense of freedom, allowing you to move forward without the burden of unrealistic expectations.

Incorporating rituals that honor your healing journey can be a meaningful practice. Rituals provide a sense of structure and intention, allowing you to acknowledge your growth and progress. This could involve lighting a candle, creating a vision board, or engaging in a reflective practice that resonates with you. Establishing rituals that celebrate your journey reinforces your commitment to self-love and healing, creating touchstones that remind you of your strength.

Embracing the concept of "progress over perfection" is essential in this journey. Understand that healing is not linear, and there will be ups and downs along the way. Celebrate the small victories and milestones, recognizing that each step forward is significant. Be gentle with yourself during moments of difficulty, allowing space for grace and understanding. By focusing on progress, you cultivate a sense of optimism that empowers you to keep moving forward.

Finding joy in small moments can significantly enhance your journey of self-love. Life is often filled with simple pleasures that can uplift your spirits. Take time to savor a cup of coffee, enjoy a walk in nature, or engage in a hobby you love. These moments of joy serve as reminders that life is rich with opportunities for happiness. By intentionally cultivating joy, you reinforce the idea that you are worthy of positive experiences and fulfillment.

Connecting with your inner child can be a powerful avenue for healing. The inner child represents the part of you that holds onto past experiences, often bearing the wounds of your youth. Engage in activities that bring you joy and spontaneity—whether it's coloring, playing games, or exploring nature. Acknowledge your inner child's feelings and needs, offering comfort and reassurance. This connection fosters healing by nurturing the parts of you that may have been overlooked or silenced.

Visualizing your ideal self can serve as a motivating force in your journey. Picture the person you aspire to be, free from the limitations of past wounds.

Create a vision of your life that embodies self-love and fulfillment. This visualization acts as a guiding light, inspiring you to take steps toward becoming that version of yourself. Use this vision as a source of motivation, reminding yourself that you have the power to shape your future.

As you navigate the intricacies of healing past wounds, cultivating a sense of hope is essential. Hope serves as a beacon, illuminating the path forward. Acknowledge that healing takes time, and trust in the process. Allow yourself to dream of a brighter future, one where you embrace self-love fully. This hopeful mindset empowers you to envision the possibilities ahead, reminding you that you are deserving of happiness and fulfillment.

Engaging in acts of kindness toward yourself can reinforce your journey of self-love. Small gestures of compassion, such as treating yourself to something special or taking a day for self-care, serve as reminders that you are worthy of love.

Chapter 6
Living Boldly, Without Apology

Walking with Confidence in Every Space

To live boldly is to embrace the essence of who you are without hesitation or fear. This kind of living involves stepping into spaces—both physical and emotional—with a sense of assurance that comes from understanding your worth and value. Walking with confidence means more than merely projecting a strong presence; it involves embodying an inner belief that you have every right to take up space in the world. The journey toward living unapologetically requires cultivating self-awareness, challenging societal norms, and developing an authentic voice that resonates with your true self.

One of the first steps toward living boldly is recognizing and dismantling the internal narratives that may hold you back. Many of us carry stories shaped by past experiences, societal expectations, or critical voices—both internal and external—that tell us we should play small. Begin by identifying these narratives. What thoughts creep in when you consider speaking up in a meeting or sharing your opinion? Reflect on moments when you felt the urge to shrink away or apologize for simply existing. Understanding these narratives is crucial, as it allows you to confront and challenge them.

Once you recognize these limiting beliefs, it's time to reframe them. Instead of internalizing negative thoughts, actively replace them with affirmations that empower you. For instance, transform "I shouldn't take up too much space" into "My voice is valuable and deserves to be heard." This practice of reframing helps cultivate a mindset of confidence and ownership. By consciously choosing to replace self-doubt with self-affirmation, you begin to reinforce the idea that you have every right to express yourself and occupy space in any environment.

Building a strong sense of self is integral to walking confidently in every space. This involves exploring your identity and values, understanding what truly matters to you. Engage in self-reflection to uncover your passions, beliefs, and strengths. Journaling can be an effective tool for this exploration. Write about your experiences, your dreams, and what brings you joy. As you clarify your identity, you create a solid foundation from which to express yourself boldly. When you know who you are and what you stand for, it becomes easier to navigate various spaces with authenticity and confidence.

Embracing vulnerability is another crucial aspect of living boldly. While it may seem counterintuitive, showing vulnerability allows you to connect more deeply with others and fosters a sense of authenticity. When you share your thoughts and feelings openly, you invite others to do the same, creating a space of trust and understanding. Embrace moments of vulnerability, whether in conversations with friends, during presentations, or while pursuing new opportunities. Each time you express your true self, you reinforce the idea that being authentic is a strength, not a weakness.

Practicing assertiveness is essential in cultivating confidence. Assertiveness is about expressing your needs and opinions clearly and respectfully. It allows you to advocate for yourself without diminishing the value of others. Start by identifying situations where you can practice assertiveness. This might involve speaking up in a meeting, setting boundaries with friends, or asserting your preferences in personal relationships. Use "I" statements to express your thoughts and feelings, such as "I feel" or "I need." This approach communicates your perspective while respecting the feelings of others, empowering you to stand firm in your beliefs and desires.

Body language plays a significant role in how we project confidence. Research shows that adopting an open and assertive posture can influence not only how others perceive you but also how you perceive yourself. Pay attention to your body language when you enter different spaces. Stand tall, maintain eye contact, and use gestures that convey openness. These nonverbal cues signal confidence, even when you may not feel it internally. Practice embodying confidence through your posture and movements, allowing your body to align with the strength you are cultivating within.

Surrounding yourself with a supportive community is a powerful way to bolster your confidence. Seek out individuals who uplift and encourage you, those who celebrate your authenticity and encourage you to pursue your dreams. Engage in conversations that inspire you and challenge you to grow. When you're in the company of people who believe in you, it becomes easier to walk boldly in every space. Your support network can serve as a reminder of your worth and potential, helping you to embrace opportunities without hesitation.

Letting go of perfectionism is another critical step in living unapologetically. Perfectionism can paralyze us, making us fear failure or judgment. Embrace the idea that imperfection is part of the human experience. Shift your focus from the desire to be flawless to the commitment to be authentic. Accept that mistakes and setbacks are opportunities for growth, not indicators of your worth. When you embrace imperfection, you liberate yourself from the constraints of comparison and self-doubt, allowing you to show up fully in every situation.

Engaging in activities that challenge you can significantly boost your confidence. Stepping outside your comfort zone allows you to discover your capabilities and expand your sense of self. This might involve taking on a new project at work, trying a new hobby, or speaking in public. Each time you push your boundaries, you reinforce your ability to navigate unfamiliar territory. Celebrate these challenges as victories, no matter how small. Each step you take toward embracing discomfort contributes to your overall confidence.

Developing a personal mantra can be a powerful tool for reinforcing your commitment to living boldly. Choose a phrase that resonates with your journey and reminds you of your strength. This mantra can serve as a touchstone during moments of self-doubt or hesitation. Repeat it to yourself regularly, especially when facing challenging situations. By embedding this affirmation into your daily life, you cultivate a mindset of empowerment and courage, helping you to walk with confidence in every space.

The practice of gratitude can also enhance your journey toward living boldly. Acknowledging the positives in your life helps shift your focus from what you lack to what you possess. Each day, take a moment to reflect on what you are grateful for, whether it's supportive relationships, personal achievements, or even small moments of joy. This practice fosters a sense of abundance, reinforcing your belief in your worthiness. When you cultivate gratitude, you develop a mindset that celebrates your experiences, making it easier to approach new opportunities with confidence.

Mindfulness plays a significant role in grounding yourself in the present moment. Often, anxiety about the future or regrets about the past can hinder our ability to walk boldly. Practicing mindfulness helps you center your thoughts, allowing you to focus on the here and now. Incorporate mindfulness techniques, such as deep breathing or meditation, into your daily routine. These practices enable you to cultivate a sense of calm and clarity, making it easier to navigate various spaces with assurance.

The power of visualization can be a transformative practice in building confidence. Take time to visualize yourself walking into different spaces with confidence and poise. Picture how you would hold yourself, how you would speak, and how you would interact with others. This mental rehearsal prepares you for real-life situations, helping you feel more at ease when facing them. Visualization reinforces your belief in your abilities, creating a positive feedback loop that encourages boldness in your actions.

Engaging in acts of self-care is vital for maintaining your confidence and well-being. When you prioritize your physical, emotional, and mental health, you cultivate a sense of self-worth that translates into your interactions with others. Establish a self-care routine that includes activities that rejuvenate and inspire you. This might involve exercise, hobbies, or simply taking time to relax. When you care for yourself, you communicate to the world that you are deserving of love and respect, empowering you to walk confidently in any space.

Learning to say "no" is a powerful skill that supports your journey of living boldly. Often, we feel pressured to please others or meet their expectations at the expense of our own well-being. Practice asserting your boundaries by saying "no" when necessary. Recognize that it's okay to prioritize your needs and desires. By setting boundaries, you create space for what truly matters to you, reinforcing your sense of agency and confidence.

Cultivating a growth mindset is instrumental in fostering a confident outlook. Embrace challenges as opportunities for learning and growth rather than as threats to your self-worth. When you approach life with a growth mindset, you develop resilience and the ability to bounce back from setbacks. Emphasize the journey of learning rather than the destination of success. This perspective encourages you to take risks, knowing that each experience contributes to your development.

Authenticity is the cornerstone of living boldly. Embrace your unique qualities and perspectives, recognizing that they are what make you stand out. Celebrate your individuality and resist the urge to conform to societal expectations. When you embrace authenticity, you attract opportunities and connections that resonate with your true self. This alignment fosters a sense of belonging and confidence, empowering you to walk boldly in every space.

Participating in activities that align with your passions and values can significantly boost your confidence. When you engage in pursuits that resonate with who you are, you reinforce your sense of purpose and fulfillment. This alignment creates a positive feedback loop, reinforcing the belief that you are capable and deserving of success. Seek out opportunities that inspire you, and allow your passions to guide your actions.

Mentorship can also play a vital role in your journey of living boldly. Seek out individuals who inspire you and can offer guidance as you navigate your path. A mentor can provide valuable insights, encouragement, and support, helping you to build confidence in your abilities. Learning from someone who has walked a similar path can provide reassurance that you are capable of achieving your goals.

The act of celebrating your achievements, no matter how small, reinforces your sense of self-worth. Create a practice of acknowledging your successes, whether they are personal or professional. This might involve keeping a journal where you record your accomplishments or sharing them with a supportive friend. By recognizing your victories, you reinforce the idea that you are deserving of recognition and that you have the capability to thrive.

Stepping into your power means embracing your voice and perspective. Your opinions and insights are valuable, and sharing them is an essential aspect of living boldly. Seek out opportunities to contribute to discussions, whether in personal relationships, professional settings, or community engagement. Your voice has the power to inspire and influence others, and expressing it with confidence reinforces your belief in your own worth.

In the journey of living boldly, remember that it's okay to seek help and support. Whether through therapy, coaching, or connecting with friends, reaching out for guidance can provide clarity and encouragement. Sharing your struggles and triumphs with others fosters a sense of connection and reminds you that you are not alone in your journey. Embracing support strengthens your resolve to live confidently and unapologetically.

Creating a personal style that reflects your authentic self can be a powerful expression of confidence. Consider how you present yourself through your clothing, accessories, and overall aesthetic. Your personal style is an extension of your identity, and embracing it can reinforce your sense of self. Choose outfits that make you feel empowered and comfortable, allowing your appearance to align with the boldness you seek to embody.

As you continue on this path of living boldly, remember that confidence is a skill that can be developed over time. Embrace the journey as one of growth, recognizing that every experience contributes to your understanding of yourself and your capabilities. Allow yourself the grace to stumble and learn, knowing that each step forward is a testament to your resilience.

Living boldly, without apology, means honoring your journey and the unique person you are becoming. Embrace the fullness of your experiences, knowing that they shape your narrative and inform your path forward. When you walk confidently in every space, you invite others to do the same, creating a ripple effect of empowerment and authenticity. In a world that often seeks to diminish individuality, standing tall in your truth becomes a radical act of self-love and self-acceptance.

Redefining Success on Your Own Terms

To live boldly is to step away from the conventional definitions of success that society often imposes. It's about understanding that your journey is uniquely yours and embracing the freedom to define what success means for you personally. In a world that frequently measures achievement through specific markers—titles, wealth, status—redefining success requires a shift in perspective. This journey invites you to explore your passions, values, and aspirations, allowing you to create a narrative that resonates with your authentic self.

Start by examining the traditional metrics of success that have been ingrained in you. Reflect on the messages you've received throughout your life—whether from family, education, media, or social circles. What were you taught to believe constitutes success? For some, it might be a prestigious job, a large house, or a certain lifestyle. For others, it might be personal fulfillment, creative expression, or meaningful relationships. Acknowledging these external influences is the first step toward freeing yourself from their confines. Recognizing how they shape your perception allows you to begin the work of redefining what success looks like for you.

The process of self-discovery is essential in this journey. Spend time reflecting on your values and priorities. What truly matters to you? Consider writing a list of your core values—these might include family, health, creativity, adventure, or community. As you identify your values, think about how they align with your current life. Are you living in accordance with what you value most? If not, what changes can you make to realign your life with your authentic self? This alignment is crucial; it lays the foundation for a definition of success that feels genuine and fulfilling.

Embracing your passions is equally important in redefining success. What activities make you feel most alive? What brings you joy and satisfaction? Pursuing your passions is not just about finding fulfillment in your work; it's about integrating what you love into your everyday life. Whether it's art, writing, cooking, or helping others, these passions serve as guiding lights in your journey. By prioritizing what you love, you create a roadmap that leads you toward a version of success that is uniquely yours.

Once you have a clearer understanding of your values and passions, it's time to envision your ideal life. Imagine a day in your life where you feel successful and fulfilled. What does that day look like? Who are you with? What activities are you engaged in? This vision serves as a powerful motivator, guiding your choices and actions as you work toward creating that reality. Visualizing your ideal life helps to clarify your goals and gives you the courage to pursue them without apology.

Setting goals that resonate with your authentic self is an important step in this process. Rather than following a prescribed path, create objectives that reflect your vision of success. These goals should align with your values and passions, driving you toward the life you want to lead. Break these goals down into actionable steps, making them more attainable. As you progress, celebrate your achievements, regardless of their size. Each step forward is a testament to your commitment to living boldly and redefining success on your own terms.

Cultivating self-compassion is a vital aspect of this journey. As you work toward your goals, it's easy to become critical of yourself, especially if you encounter setbacks or obstacles. Remember that growth is not linear. Be gentle with yourself during challenging times, recognizing that each experience contributes to your overall development. Practicing self-compassion allows you to acknowledge your struggles without judgment, fostering resilience and perseverance in your pursuit of success.

Surrounding yourself with supportive individuals can significantly impact your journey. Seek out friends, mentors, or communities that uplift you and encourage your authentic expression. Engage in conversations that inspire growth and challenge societal norms. The company you keep can influence your mindset, helping you to cultivate a culture of support and accountability. Share your goals and aspirations with these individuals, inviting them to be part of your journey. Their encouragement can serve as a powerful motivator as you redefine success.

Navigating societal expectations can be one of the most challenging aspects of this journey. It's easy to feel pressure to conform to traditional ideas of success, particularly from family and peers. Acknowledge these pressures but remember that they do not define your worth or your path. Practice assertiveness in communicating your values and goals to others. It's essential to express your choices with confidence, reinforcing your commitment to living life on your terms. This assertiveness can help to create space for honest conversations about your aspirations, allowing others to understand and support your journey.

Engaging in self-reflection is a powerful practice that allows you to continually reassess your definition of success. Schedule regular check-ins with yourself, asking questions about your feelings, goals, and progress. Are you still aligned with your values? Are your passions evolving? This practice encourages you to remain adaptable and open to change, ensuring that your definition of success grows with you. Life is dynamic, and your vision may shift as you navigate different experiences. Embracing this fluidity is essential in maintaining a sense of authenticity.

As you redefine success, consider the importance of balance in your life. It's easy to become consumed by the pursuit of goals, but neglecting other areas can lead to burnout and dissatisfaction. Strive for a holistic approach, where you prioritize your well-being, relationships, and passions alongside your professional aspirations. Balance allows you to cultivate a richer, more fulfilling life, where each aspect contributes to your overall sense of success. Reflect on how you can incorporate self-care, leisure, and connection into your daily routine. This balance reinforces the idea that success is not solely defined by achievements but by the quality of your experiences.

Practicing gratitude is another powerful tool for redefining success. Regularly acknowledge the positive aspects of your life, no matter how small. Gratitude shifts your focus from what you lack to what you have, fostering a sense of abundance and fulfillment. Consider keeping a gratitude journal where you record moments of joy, achievements, and the support you receive from others. This practice cultivates a mindset that celebrates your journey, reinforcing the notion that success is multifaceted and deeply personal.

Engaging in activities that push you outside your comfort zone is crucial for personal growth. Embrace challenges that scare you, whether they involve taking on a new project, speaking in public, or pursuing a passion you've long neglected. Each time you step into discomfort, you expand your sense of self and redefine what you are capable of achieving. This process not only enhances your confidence but also reinforces the understanding that success often lies beyond the boundaries of familiarity.

Letting go of comparison is essential in your journey of living boldly. It's easy to fall into the trap of measuring your worth against others, especially in the age of social media where curated lives are often presented. Remember that everyone's journey is unique, and comparing yourself to others only detracts from your own growth. Focus on your path, celebrating your accomplishments and the progress you make. Surround yourself with reminders of your unique journey, whether through affirmations, visual cues, or inspiring quotes. This practice reinforces the idea that your success is not contingent on anyone else's narrative.

Developing resilience is vital as you navigate the challenges that come with redefining success. Life is filled with uncertainties, and setbacks are inevitable. Cultivate a mindset that embraces adversity as an opportunity for growth. When faced with obstacles, remind yourself that they do not diminish your worth or potential. Each challenge is a stepping stone toward your goals. By fostering resilience, you empower yourself to bounce back stronger and more determined, reinforcing your commitment to living boldly.

Engaging in continuous learning is a powerful way to redefine success. Embrace a mindset of curiosity, seeking out new experiences, knowledge, and perspectives. This commitment to lifelong learning expands your horizons and enriches your journey. Whether through formal education, workshops, or self-study, invest in your personal development. Each new skill or insight contributes to your sense of accomplishment and reinforces the understanding that success is about growth, not perfection.

Creating a vision board can serve as a tangible representation of your redefined success. Visualize your goals, aspirations, and the life you wish to create. Use images, words, and symbols that resonate with your vision. Display this board in a space where you can see it daily, allowing it to serve as a source of inspiration and motivation. This visual reminder reinforces your commitment to your authentic journey, helping you to stay focused on what truly matters.

The importance of self-advocacy cannot be overstated. As you redefine success, learn to advocate for yourself and your needs. This involves communicating your goals to others, whether in professional or personal settings. Practice articulating your aspirations clearly and confidently. Self-advocacy empowers you to pursue opportunities that align with your vision, reinforcing your sense of agency and control over your life.

Celebrating your journey is crucial as you redefine success. Acknowledge the milestones you achieve along the way, no matter how small. Create rituals to mark your accomplishments, whether through reflection, sharing with others, or treating yourself to something special. This practice not only reinforces your progress but also cultivates a sense of gratitude for the journey itself. Each celebration serves as a reminder of your resilience and commitment to living boldly.

Engaging in community service or giving back can also enhance your understanding of success. Contributing to causes that resonate with your values fosters a sense of connection and purpose. It reinforces the idea that success is not solely about personal achievement but also about making a positive impact on the world around you. Seek out opportunities to volunteer or support initiatives that inspire you. This engagement broadens your perspective and enriches your understanding of fulfillment.

Developing a strong sense of intuition is another critical aspect of redefining success. Trusting your instincts allows you to make choices that align with your authentic self. Pay attention to how certain situations or decisions make you feel. Your intuition can serve as a valuable guide, helping you navigate the complexities of life and make choices that resonate with your values. Cultivating this connection with your inner voice enhances your confidence in pursuing your unique path.

As you navigate this journey of redefining success, remember that it is not a destination but a continuous process. Embrace the evolving nature of your aspirations and be open to change. Life experiences, relationships, and personal growth will influence your understanding of success over time. Stay adaptable and willing to reassess your goals, ensuring they align with who you are becoming.

Living boldly, without apology, is about embracing your authentic self and creating a life that reflects your true values and passions. It requires the courage to challenge societal expectations and pursue your unique path with confidence. By redefining success on your terms, you empower yourself to live a life that is deeply fulfilling and aligned with your essence. Embrace the journey, celebrating each step toward your version of success, and inspire others to do the same. In a world that often seeks to impose its standards, your commitment to living unapologetically becomes a powerful act of self-love and authenticity.

Conclusion

Embracing your authentic self is a profound journey filled with self-discovery, vulnerability, and empowerment. Throughout this exploration, we've navigated various facets of self-love, from redefining success to celebrating uniqueness, understanding the power of self-expression, and cultivating meaningful relationships. Each of these elements plays a crucial role in constructing a life that resonates with who you truly are, free from the weight of societal expectations and comparison.

Self-love is not a one-time achievement; it's an ongoing practice, a daily commitment to nurture and honor your true self. This journey invites you to peel back the layers, to confront the fears and doubts that may have held you captive. As you delve deeper into the essence of who you are, it becomes clearer that self-acceptance and compassion are foundational to living unapologetically.

The act of redefining success is transformative. Moving away from traditional metrics—such as titles, possessions, or status—allows you to forge a path aligned with your values and passions. Success, in its truest form, becomes about fulfillment, joy, and authenticity. This redefinition is not just a personal revolution; it inspires others to reflect on their own lives, fostering a community where everyone is encouraged to pursue their unique dreams.

Engaging in self-expression is a powerful means of asserting your identity. Finding your voice in a world filled with noise can feel daunting, but each time you express your thoughts, feelings, and creativity, you reinforce your worth. This authenticity draws others to you, creating connections based on honesty and vulnerability. Relationships thrive when founded on mutual respect and understanding, allowing you to build honest connections that support your growth.

As you learn to set boundaries with grace, you create a protective space for your well-being. Boundaries are not barriers but rather guidelines that foster healthy interactions. They empower you to engage fully in your relationships while maintaining your sense of self. Embracing this aspect of self-love ensures that you prioritize your needs and desires, cultivating deeper and more meaningful connections.

Celebrating your uniqueness is an essential part of this journey. In a world that often pushes conformity, recognizing and embracing your differences can feel revolutionary. Your quirks, your passions, and your perspectives are what make you who you are. By celebrating these attributes, you not only honor yourself but also encourage others to do the same. This celebration of individuality fosters a culture of acceptance and appreciation, allowing everyone to thrive in their authenticity.

The practice of self-compassion is vital. Life's journey is filled with ups and downs, and it's easy to be harsh on yourself when things don't go as planned. Learning to treat yourself with kindness during moments of struggle transforms your relationship with failure. Rather than seeing setbacks as a reflection of your worth, they become stepping stones toward growth and resilience. This shift in mindset is a cornerstone of self-love, helping you to bounce back stronger and more determined.

Navigating self-doubt is another significant aspect of embracing your authentic power. Recognizing that self-doubt is a universal experience allows you to confront it with empathy rather than judgment. Each time you challenge that inner critic, you strengthen your self-worth. Remember that confidence is built through action, and stepping outside of your comfort zone is where true growth occurs. The more you push against those doubts, the more you solidify your belief in your capabilities.

Living boldly, without apology, encourages you to engage fully with life. It's about stepping into spaces with confidence and owning your narrative. When you walk into a room knowing your worth, you not only uplift yourself but inspire others to embrace their authenticity. This ripple effect creates a powerful movement toward collective self-love and acceptance.

As you navigate your path, seek out communities that resonate with your values. Surrounding yourself with supportive individuals amplifies your journey. Engage in conversations that challenge societal norms, share your aspirations, and celebrate your progress. Together, you can foster a culture of empowerment, reminding each other that your journeys are valid and worthy of celebration.

Reflection is a powerful tool in this journey. Regularly checking in with yourself helps you stay aligned with your evolving goals and values. Life is fluid, and your understanding of yourself may shift over time. Embrace this evolution with curiosity, allowing your experiences to shape your path. Your willingness to adapt and reassess your definition of self-love ensures that you remain true to yourself.

Cultivating gratitude enhances your journey toward self-love. By acknowledging the abundance in your life, you shift your focus from what you lack to what you have. This practice fosters a sense of fulfillment and joy, reminding you that success is not solely about achievements but also about appreciating the present moment. Create rituals that cultivate gratitude in your daily life, reinforcing the understanding that every experience contributes to your overall journey.

Embrace your journey as a unique narrative, one that deserves to be told and celebrated. Your experiences, both triumphs and challenges, shape who you are and offer invaluable lessons. Sharing your story with others can create connections and foster a sense of community. By opening up about your journey, you invite others to do the same, creating a space for vulnerability and understanding.

As you continue to walk this path, remember the importance of self-advocacy. Speak up for your needs, desires, and aspirations. Your voice matters, and advocating for yourself reinforces your belief in your worth. Whether in personal or professional settings, learning to articulate your goals with confidence empowers you to pursue opportunities that align with your authentic self.

Commit to lifelong learning as a means of growth. Embrace a mindset of curiosity, seeking out new experiences, knowledge, and perspectives. This dedication to self-improvement enriches your journey, allowing you to expand your horizons continually. As you learn and evolve, you reinforce the understanding that success is a journey, not a destination.

Ultimately, living unapologetically is about honoring yourself in all your complexity. It requires courage to embrace who you are and to stand firm in your values and aspirations. As you embark on this journey, celebrate each step, acknowledging your growth and resilience. Surround yourself with love, kindness, and understanding, both from yourself and those around you.

The journey toward self-love and authenticity is a profound one, filled with rich experiences and invaluable lessons. Embrace the fullness of your identity and recognize the beauty in your uniqueness. Allow yourself to grow, to stumble, and to rise again. As you navigate the complexities of life, remain committed to your truth, honoring the **powerful** and authentic being you are. In doing so, you invite others to join you on this journey, creating a world where everyone can celebrate their own unapologetic selves.

Appendix

This appendix serves as a collection of resources, practices, and reflections designed to support you on your journey toward embracing your authentic power and self-love. Each section offers tools to help you deepen your understanding and foster a stronger connection with yourself.

1. Daily Self-Love Practices

Establishing a routine of self-love can significantly impact your well-being. Here are some practices you can incorporate into your daily life:

- **Morning Affirmations**: Begin each day with positive affirmations that resonate with you. Examples include:

- "I am worthy of love and respect."
- "I embrace my uniqueness and celebrate my journey."

- **Gratitude Journaling**: Set aside a few minutes each day to write down three things you are grateful for. This practice can shift your focus from what you lack to what you have.
- **Mindful Moments**: Practice mindfulness through meditation or deep-breathing exercises. Take a few minutes to center yourself, focusing on your breath and being present in the moment.
- **Acts of Kindness**: Engage in small acts of kindness towards yourself and others. Whether it's treating yourself to your favorite coffee or complimenting a friend, these gestures can foster a sense of connection and joy.

2. Reflection Questions

Self-reflection is crucial for personal growth. Consider these questions to deepen your understanding of yourself:

- What are my core values, and how do they influence my decisions?
- What passions bring me joy, and how can I incorporate them into my daily life?
- How do I define success, and does that definition resonate with my authentic self?
- In what areas of my life do I need to set boundaries to protect my well-being?
- What fears or doubts hold me back, and how can I challenge them?

3. Books and Resources for Further Exploration

Expand your knowledge and understanding of self-love and authenticity through these recommended readings and resources:

- **"The Gifts of Imperfection" by Brené Brown**: A guide to embracing vulnerability and cultivating self-worth.
- **"You Are a Badass" by Jen Sincero**: A motivational book that encourages readers to embrace their inner power.
- **"The Untethered Soul" by Michael A. Singer**: Explores the concept of self and consciousness, encouraging readers to connect with their true selves.
- **Podcasts**:
    - **"Unlocking Us" with Brené Brown**: Conversations that explore what it means to be human.
    - **"The Minimalists"**: Discussions on living a meaningful life with less.

4. Supportive Communities and Organizations

Engaging with supportive communities can enhance your journey. Here are some organizations and online platforms to consider:

- **Meetup**: Join local groups focused on self-improvement, creativity, or mindfulness.
- **Self-Compassion.org**: Resources and tools for cultivating self-compassion.
- **Therapy and Counseling**: Consider seeking professional support to navigate your journey. Websites like Psychology Today can help you

find therapists in your area.

5. Creative Expression Ideas

Engaging in creative activities can be a powerful form of self-expression. Explore these ideas to channel your creativity:

- **Art Journaling**: Combine writing and visual art to express your thoughts and emotions.
- **Writing Prompts**: Use prompts to explore your feelings and experiences. Examples:
    - "What does self-love look like for me?"
    - "Write a letter to my younger self."
- **Dance or Movement**: Use movement as a form of self-expression. Whether through dance, yoga, or simply walking, allow your body to communicate your feelings.

6. Goal-Setting Framework

Setting meaningful goals can guide you toward your authentic life. Consider using the SMART criteria to define your objectives:

- **Specific**: Clearly outline what you want to achieve.
- **Measurable**: Determine how you will track your progress.
- **Achievable**: Ensure your goal is realistic and attainable.
- **Relevant**: Align your goal with your values and passions.
- **Time-bound**: Set a deadline to create a sense of urgency.

7. Affirmation Cards

Creating affirmation cards can be a fun and motivating practice. Here's how to make your own:

1. Gather materials: Index cards, markers, and decorative items.
2. Write affirmations that resonate with you on each card.
3. Decorate the cards to reflect your personality.
4. Place them in visible areas as daily reminders of your worth.

8. Personal Development Plan

Develop a personal growth plan by following these steps:

1. **Identify Areas for Growth**: Reflect on aspects of your life you wish to improve.
2. **Set Goals**: Use the SMART criteria to define clear objectives.
3. **Create an Action Plan**: Outline the steps you will take to achieve your goals.
4. **Review and Adjust**: Regularly assess your progress and adjust your plan as needed.

9. Mindfulness and Meditation Resources

Incorporating mindfulness into your daily life can enhance your self-love journey. Consider these resources:

- **Apps**:
    - **Headspace**: Offers guided meditations and mindfulness exercises.
    - **Calm**: Provides sleep stories, meditations, and relaxation techniques.
- **Online Courses**: Explore platforms like Coursera or Udemy for mindfulness and meditation courses.

Don't miss out!

Visit the website below and you can sign up to receive emails whenever Leon McCoy publishes a new book. There's no charge and no obligation.

https://books2read.com/r/B-A-DBRMC-HESFF

BOOKS 2 READ

Connecting independent readers to independent writers.

Also by Leon McCoy

Unshakable: Build Lasting Confidence And Conquer Your Fears
Killing Lust Is Easy: A Journey Worth Taking
Rewiring Your Brain: A 100-Day Journey to Overcome Porn Addiction
Silence Is Power: How Quiet Leaders Dominate The Loud World
Beyond First Impressions: The Essential Guide To Building Meaningful Relationships
Mastering Your Potential: Breaking The Chains Of Limiting Habits
Unapologetically Me: Embrace Your Authentic Power and Self Love

Milton Keynes UK
Ingram Content Group UK Ltd.
UKHW021047111124
451035UK00017B/1436